"Most of us think of water as a liquid . . ."
—Thomson King

ON WATER

ON WATER

Thomas Farber

THE ECCO PRESS

Several sections of this book have first appeared in a different
form as a chapbook from Okeanos Press in Berkeley,
California. An essay drawn from it also appeared in *A World
Between Waves*, and other essays in the *Journal of the Contemporary
Pacific* and *Chaminade Literary Review*.

THE ECCO PRESS
100 West Broad Street
Hopewell, New Jersey 08525
Published simultaneously in Canada by
Penguin Books Canada Ltd., Ontario
Printed in the United States of America

Library of Congress Cataloging-in-Publication Data
Farber, Thomas, 1944–
On water / by Thomas Farber.
p.   cm.
1. Farber, Thomas, 1944–   —Homes and haunts—Hawaii.
2. Farber, Thomas, 1944–   —Homes and haunts—California.
3. Authors, American—20th century—biography.
4. Aquatic sports—California.
5. Aquatic sports—Hawaii.
6. Water. I. Title.
PS3556.A64Z466   1994
813'.54—dc20
[B]   93-41183
ISBN 0-88001-358-3
ISBN 0-88001-459-8 (paperback)

Designed by Debby Jay
Photograph by Wayne Levin

The text of this book is set in Centaur

9 8 7 6 5 4 3 2 1

FIRST PAPERBACK EDITION

For Hsu Yin Peh and Hsu Li

THE AUTHOR gratefully acknowledges assistance given by Chester Aaron, John Anson, Joel August, Garry Bennett, Patrick Caldwell, Vicki Chang, Shannon Chang-Eaton, Dan Chow, Denis Clifford, Bob Crane, Fred Curtice, Gavan Daws, Joe DeGrazia, Daniel Duane, Jim Duane, Katherine and Richard Duane, Tony and Betsy Dubovsky, Epi Enari, Marion Faber, Larry Foster, Jack and Marty Ford, Leah Garchik, Dan Hammer, Stephen Hannaford, Epeli and Barbara Hau'ofa, Vilsoni Hereniko, Pat Hereniko, Louis Herman, Millicent Horton, Jim Houston, Eric Johnson, Hilda Johnston, Bob Kiste, Diana Landau, Jeremy Larner, Wayne Levin, Leo Litwak, Pio Manoa, Nikki Martin, Kathy Matsueda, Pat Matsueda, Joseph Matthews, Clemi McLaren, David and Else Miller, Fred Miller, Stephen Mitchell, Victoria Nelson, Susan Nunes, John and Nathalie O'Carroll, Robert Pinsky, Alix Pitcher, Phil Polakoff, Bob and Betty Ann Sallee, William Santis, Judith Shepard, Tom Steffan, Subramani, Bernard Taper, Carolyn Tipton, David Vardy, Joseph Veramu, Geoffrey White, and Peter Yedidia.

Special thanks to William B. Goodman, waterman; to Stewart Heller, who urged me to find an island; to Frank Stewart, who shared his knowledge of natural history writing; and to Sara

Bershtel, for her support of the finished manuscript. Thanks also to the Committee for the International Exchange of Scholars for the award that allowed my travel in the South Pacific, and to the East-West Center in Honolulu, which took me in as a Visiting Fellow.

T.F.
Berkeley, California
Honolulu, Hawai'i

ON WATER

"... The rip pulled us toward the lava at the north
            end of the beach,
and we had to swim hard to stay there ...

We ducked the biggest waves that caught
us inside. A quick breath, then down to kick along
            the
sand toward the blue haze outside, the waves
            cracking, pressure
from the white water hissing over us, a cold shadow.
            We surfaced
on the other side, looked at each other and laughed,
surprised again to have made it into the sunlight and
            air."

—TINO RAMIREZ

CALL ME QUEEQUEG. Out once more to surf at Tongg's,
line-up perhaps two hundred and fifty yards offshore. Storm
clouds above the Ko'olaus and over past the cathedral-like mass
of Diamond Head, rain beards—gray, grayer—dropping from

the low sky, and then suddenly a squall is on us, boards and riders blown downwind, paddling hard into the chop and spray just to hold position. A simultaneous abrupt absence of light: furrows, folds, flanks, buttresses, and crevices of Diamond Head obliterated, waves almost black. *Wai* and *kai*, fresh and salt, song of the water planet (Earth-the-misnomer). But then, faster than we can adjust to the change, the sun's reappeared, the water's jade green. And, saying he has to get home, Wendell paddles 'Ewa toward Sans Souci Beach.

Wendell. "Local" Chinese, in his late fifties/early sixties. Former airline mechanic, grew up in Honolulu. The year before, Wendell arrived one morning—spontaneously generated as if summoned by the waves—out at Tongg's riding high on his massive ten footer, paddling easily, surgical tubing around his waist as a leash. Unorthodox, but effective. No one else there that day, we sat bobbing on the swell, shafts of the boards erect before us, thick plume of smoke rising from the cane fields down toward the Wai'anae range. Watches and clocks irrelevant mechanisms of measure here, time organizing itself into sets and lulls, sets and lulls, Wendell speaking of the change in the color of the water since he was a kid, the loss of clarity/seaweed/shellfish. We sat silent for a while, gently rising and falling, Diamond Head always again compelling our attention, like the landform obsessing Richard Dreyfuss in *Close Encounters of the Third Kind.* Sometimes, clouds scudding behind the volcano's vast bulk as we lifted and dropped, sometimes it seemed we were the fixed point, Diamond Head that must be moving.

WATER REMAINS A CHAOS," Ivan Illich writes, "until a creative story interprets its seeming equivocation . . . Most myths of creation have as one of their main tasks the conjuring of water. This conjuring always seems to be a division . . . the creator, by dividing the waters, makes space for creation." Illich also writes that "to keep one's bearing when exploring water, one must not lose sight of its dual nature." Deep and shallow, life-giving and murderous, etc. etc.

Melville, for instance, reading the mystery of both sea and terra firma: "consider them . . . and do you not find a strange analogy to something in yourself? For as this appalling ocean surrounds the verdant land, so in the soul of man there lies an insular Tahiti, full of peace and joy, but encompassed by all the horrors of the half known life. God keep thee! Push not off from that isle, thou canst never return!"

Reading water. "Water represents the unconscious," says the psychologist at the party. The surface the boundary between consciousness and unconsciousness. Water in this view thus a form of seductive regression, representing the purely instinctive. As Heraclitus cautioned, "It is fatal for the soul to dissolve in water."

For instance, naturalist Ann Zwinger, entering the "peaceful, cradling ocean," then looking up from below at the surface, "a silken tent in the underwater wind, gray blue with moving ovals." Dazzled by the "interlocking lozenges of light," she writes: "how simple it is for those who pivot or rasp, supported and fed, adrift in an infinite womb, bathed in a life-support medium full of needed nutrients, needing less to eat than their land-based counterparts, less plagued by temperature fluctuations and dessication, no need to heat their blood, filled with body fluids with the same osmotic pressure, so needing less protective covering to separate them from an alien atmosphere, suspended easily in this friendly bath without having to battle the incessant pull of gravity."

Or consider the vision of author Joan Ocean, who in seeking a name that conveyed "no male lineage," took on the first word that came to her. As she notes in *Dolphin Connection*, it "was easy to spell, easy for other people to remember, unusual." What's in a name? It was not until seven years later that she first experienced a "symbiotic love for the ocean . . . I accepted completely my personal connection to it, and my responsibility to preserve and respect all of the vast life forms that resided within it." This epiphany came "by 'absorption,' " after she had for the first time been in the water with (captive) dolphins. Soon, Joan Ocean wanted to be a dolphin, which for her meant "to be weightless and buoyant," to "move within the changing currents of water, to feel the earth turn, to slide on the waves, and be surrounded by the varied and unique concerts of sea animals. To play in the sparkling shafts of sunlight and bubbles, to feel the pull of the moon and the stars . . . to have seventy percent of the planet as your intimate and cozy home."

Ocean does not mention, however, that dolphins are predators—of squid, lantern fish, shrimp, etc.—and that they have their own predators, including the eighteen-inch "cookie cutter shark," which uses suction to extract large discs of dolphin flesh. More, deep-water dolphins school because it increases their capacity to protect themselves and/or to feed successfully. Lone Ranger dolphins, James Dean dolphins? Apparently not in the Pacific. Nonetheless, Joan Ocean has experienced "commingling with particles of the water," has come to believe that telepathic interspecies messages can be "conveyed on this air-water conduit." (In Rodman's "The Dolphin Papers," it is recorded in cetacean lore that a few human beings will one day make contact with the dolphins, but in one version of this cetacean legend, apparently, the humans never return to their own kind. In others, they return to be imprisoned as lunatics, or, alternately, to implement either a bloodless coup d'état or an "insurrection of all the beasts," which eliminates humans as "irredeemably depraved and dangerous to the planet.")

Liquid eyes. For Claudel, "that unexplored pool of liquid light which God put in the depths of our being." And, by extension: "water is the gaze of the earth, its instrument for looking at time." Water perhaps also being the earth's instrument for looking at us. And/or, our instrument for us to look at ourselves. As Melville wrote, Narcissus could not grab hold of the "tormenting, mild image he saw in the fountain, plunged into it and was drowned. But that same image we ourselves see in all rivers and oceans. It is the image of the ungraspable phantom of life." Put another way, the story of Narcissus suggests that the images of the self we see in water are not only seductive, but lethal.

Reading water. Dylan Thomas' "carol-singing sea," for example. Or that sentient, conscious ocean in Lem's science fiction novel *Solaris,* capable of diagnosing the hearts of the scientists observing it and, even, of creating for them incarnations of their hungers. One studies the ocean on the planet Solaris, then, only at enormous risk. And always, of course, there are the limits of perception: the ocean on Solaris, Lem seems to be saying, is beyond human ken, whatever the human yearning for "Contact." (Poet Robinson Jeffers, looking west from Carmel, for years studied "the hill of water" which is "half the / planet: this dome, this half-globe, this bulging / Eyeball of water" with "eyelids that / never close", what Jeffers termed "the staring unsleeping / Eye of the earth." And, he concluded, "what it watches is not our wars.")

Reading water. "To describe a wave analytically," Calvino wrote, "to translate its every movement into words, one would have to invent a new vocabulary and perhaps also a new grammar and a new syntax, or else employ a system of notation like a musical score." Making a start, Pablo Neruda says, "teach us to see the sea wave by wave." Not a bad aspiration, though Neruda himself is quick to figurative language: the ocean's "gifts and dooms," the "spent comet" of the wave's "scorn and desire." The need of the poet, like Lem's scientists, to make Contact. To name the qualities of even Earth's ocean, Lem seems to be arguing, thus reveals our hungers. Takes us to the limits of our capacities. And beyond.

T HE ONLY RECORDED STATEMENT of Thales, the presocratic: "Everything is water, water is all."

Los Angeles: weekend summer afternoon at the Ganges off Santa Monica Beach. Parking lots and freeways, jammed. North and south as far as the eye can see, hundreds, thousands of people of various races and ethnicities being lifted in the curl of the breaking wave. Pause; gather; surge; drop.

Hours and hours in the sun, day finally waning. Nearby, a woman with blonde hair and enormous blue eyes begins to glow in the dusk, gaining force in the waning light like some summer planet moving toward the horizon. On her back, propped up on her elbows, staring out to sea. Giving me a smile each time I pass, coming in from yet another session of porpoising in the shore break, a nod as if of approval: as if only the two of us can comprehend the secret of this light, these waves.

To turn one's back on the land, to enter the proximate wilderness of the sea, sets coming in from forever. The familiar blast of mist as a wave drops down on a pocket of trapped air. Surf beating on, vaporizing over, the reef. And what's being left behind as one pushes off? Flickering TV light in the windows of the highrises along the shore at sunset, testimony to the human capacity—need—to rival and miniaturize the larger creation. NFL football, Oprah, Brokaw, Pavarotti. The community of modern man, but in Hawai'i there is a sadness on the land. The drumbeat of development, future shock, a pace of environmental change faster and more extensive than even *Homo sapiens* can absorb. Yet one more golf course/development/resort, home-grown legislators cashing out, cashing in. "Straddling the Tropic of Cancer admidst the trackless waters of the North Pacific," writes Patrick Kirch, "the Hawaiian chain is the most isolated archipelago in the world . . . Once a colonizing plant or animal had managed to pass through 'the sieves of overseas transport' . . . it more likely than not found the environment free of competitors. A process of adaptive radiation and speciation followed." Thus the awesome impact of man's imported plants, animals, and farming: for instance, something like half the species of Hawaiian land birds became extinct during the per-haps two thousand–year Polynesian era before European contact. (Numbers: 70 percent of nonmigrant native birds, 50 percent of native insects, and hundreds of species of native plants are now extinct; 50 percent of the survivors are candidates for the federal endangered species list.)

Radiation, speciation. In 1916 a three-year-old elephant, Daisy, captured in what was then Rhodesia, made a twenty thousand–mile sea voyage to arrive at Honolulu. Though a sensation at first, in time Daisy became difficult to handle, was chained to trees for weeks at a time. By 1933, her keepers feared Daisy, were reluctant to feed her or clean her area. When the public protested a plan to execute Daisy, her original keeper said he'd care for her without salary. Three days after he resumed work, however, Daisy picked him up with her trunk and gored him with her tusks. Police marksmen then shot and killed her.

Radiation, speciation. Humans, those late arrivals, also an adaptive species. But native Hawaiians? The "Hawaiian renais-sance" that began in the 1970s: to talk of native Hawaiians is perforce to acknowledge nightmares of the not-so-distant past. ("The death of a culture," argues Victoria Nelson, "like the death of a star, lasts longer than anyone can possibly imagine. The sadness, the echoes and ambiguities, persist for hundreds of years.") Not quite the death of Hawaiian culture in the nine-teenth century, but close: according to David Stannard, the native Hawaiian population fell from more than five hundred thousand to forty thousand in the one hundred years after first contact with the west, "bodies eaten alive by the white man's venereal syphilis, consumed by the fires of his influenza, gored by his tuberculosis." Whites, for Stannard, the real cannibals of the Pacific. This karma, these ghosts. Such violation, human and environmental. *Extinction is forever,* says a sticker on the rent-a-car.

Radiation, speciation. Like a number of the migrants who now come to Hawai'i, who fear a grim future for the islands, who feel they know how to parse the past—like them I arrive, depart, and arrive again on a Boeing 747, that leviathan of man's technology. The airplane meal is offered to me too, though I usually bring my own food. A pure spirit—I may be reading up on ecology during the in-flight film—I'm further blessed with *Homo sapiens'* most peculiar gift, the capacity to exempt myself from what I most deplore.

THERE WAS A TIME, of course, when there was no water on Earth. But then, above the inferno, core of this developing planet, replacing a cloud of carbon monoxide, methane, and ammonia, an atmosphere marked by hydrogen and carbon dioxide formed, water appearing as vapor. Finally, the Earth's crust slowly cooling, this vapor condensed; for many millions of years, it rained. (The source of this water is still a question: there were ice particles within the interstellar cloud, also water from the comets, themselves mostly ice.)

Earth, it happens, is both large enough—has enough mass— to retain its water and atmospheric gases (unlike the Moon, for instance), and is far enough from the sun not to have them burned away (which allowed liquid water to remain here the time needed for life to develop in the oceans).

Consider also the following:

- The water created 3 billion years ago is still in existence.
- 97 percent of world's water is in the oceans, 2 percent in ice. Water is the most abundant liquid; water completely covers 71 percent of the globe.
- Water is a "scientific freak," denser as a liquid than as a

solid—most solids sink in their own liquid, that is, expand when they melt—and is the only chemical compound found as solid, liquid, and gas. Were it a "normal" compound, it would occur only as a gas given Earth's surface temperatures and pressures.

- Water is formless but never loses its identity, is incompressible but offers no resistance to a change of shape.
- A powerful reagent, water can dissolve any other substance. Also, since water is the most universal of solvents, we never see pure water in its liquid form.
- As noted above, breaking the rules of physics, water is not more dense as temperature falls—ice would sink otherwise—but also, breaking the rules of chemistry, water is both an acid and a base, and so can react chemically with itself or anything else.
- Water has no nutritive value, but is the major constituent of all living things.
- In its aspects as solid, liquid, and gas—all the possible forms of matter we know—water is both the defining feature of life on our planet and yet in constant flux. Nothing is lost in these transformations, however—the water in our blood will be cloud one day, was glacier eons ago—which makes water a good proof of the most essential laws of our universe.

The *Encyclopaedia Britannica*, 15th edition, observes, "Many theories have been developed to explain the structure of pure liquid water; some can account for most of water's peculiar properties, but none can account for all." For Lyall Watson, it is not simply that water is physically and chemically unique. "It may be necessary," he writes, "to think of water as an organism in its own right, as a creature that metabolizes . . ." (Walt Whitman's water that "sports and sings." And that sentient ocean in Lem's *Solaris,* a "Metamorph" which weighs "some seven hundred billion tons." Or water as Tom Robbins's intrepid traveler through four dimensions: "It has even been said that human beings were invented by water as a device for transporting itself from one place to another.")

I FOUND MANY WAYS of being wet . . .," writes Victoria Nelson in *My Time in Hawaii*. "Most of all I found the ocean, *moana*, in all its shapes: the calm, quiet sea (*kai mālie, kai mālino, kai malolo, kai hoʻolulu, kai pu, kai wahine, kai kalamania, kaiolohia*), the strong sea (*kai koʻo, kai kāne, kai nui, kai nuʻu, ʻōkaikai*), the rough or raging sea (*kai pupule, kai puʻeone, kai akua*), the deep sea (*kai hohonu, kai ʻau, kai hōʻeʻe, kai lú heʻe*), the place where sea and land meet (*ʻae kai*), the sea almost surrounded by land (*kai hāloko*), the eight seas around the Hawaiian islands (*nākai ʻewalu*)."

Pelagic: of or pertaining to the seas or oceans. Call me pelagic. Rocking in the swell, hour after hour, a lulling to and fro. Drawn to the wave, lifted, thrown. The wave sucking up, sucking up, rising, rising. Pull, lift, push. In time, the system tunes to the surge. The erotic pleasure, on shore even hours later, of carrying this essential rhythm in blood and bone.

Out so long that one (almost) forgets to come in. Floating toward shore, finally, like a jellyfish before the wind. Arriving in the ebb and flow, draw and wash, like a sailor clinging to a spar. Like King Arthur on his bier floating downriver to the sea.

TOURISTS ON THE BEACH, nearly nude, oil-smeared, like seals in the sun, their skimpy bathing suits sporting gaudy neon colors rivaling the hues of the underwater world.

Heading out, breaking the surface. Going under. All that's above immediately washed away. *This* world sharpening the reflexes: what's that shape? That possibility? Big fish/little fish. The evolutionary path not taken. Some fish, seeing my approach, flick a fin and are gone, masters of understatement, while others flee as if the Devil himself is in pursuit. Several herds of *manini* (surgeonfish) go by, all stripes and eyes. Noticing two large parrotfish off to the side and behind me, I turn toward shore, wait for a breaking wave, and ride in on them, fast. No spear, no gun: just teasing.

Chugging onward, past a group of dazzling Moorish idols. Sight of them evoking, demanding an answer to, the question that has long obsessed icthyologists—the purpose of piscine coloration. To establish territory, confuse predators, facilitate breeding, aid schooling (which has survival value)? Good theories all, reasoned, sound (if nonetheless drab compared to such opulent display).

Heading farther out, and, suddenly, seeing to the bottom of

a deep trench, water quite clear, feeling a *frisson* of vertigo: Hey, a person could fall all the way down. Comes the thought, What holds one up?

Out at the reef, I stare at a freckled hawkfish perched in plain view on a coral head as if fully camouflaged, though its colors fail to make it look even like a fish trying to look like coral. Eyes twitching, it refuses to budge. Called *po'o pa'a* (stubborn) by Hawaiians, it finally moves off—in irritation, piqued?—when I hover. Only later does it dawn on me that the hawkfish's strategy might have been not so much to hide as to attract.

A boxfish, seeing my approach, simply stares, as if it well knows that with armor and poison it has little to fear from the likes of me. Rotating, I see a fish with a broad face, tubby, blue with white spots, a North Sea double-ender, sturdy, with huge panda button eyes, all kinds of improbable small eggbeater fins whirling away. "Come out, come out," I say without speaking, "I just want to see you better," now sounding to myself like the wolf in *Little Red Riding Hood*. "Come on," I continue, "I'm not into *sashimi*—tonight," and laugh into the mouthpiece of my snorkel. Some joke. Making me look around, suddenly, for any large dorsal fins . . .

Lured onward by more parrotfish, as if by sirens, into the gloaming. Just wondering where the morays are when—*arggh*—there's one right below, mouth open wide as I pass over, lots of sharp teeth, very reptilian. Message to the cerebral cortex going back to data programmed in there say 25,000 years ago. Worse, this moray is rather far out of its hole, swaying like a cobra, out to its bellybutton so to speak. Making me nervous, though of course morays *never* attack unless disturbed on their turf. And yet. What if just one of them forgets the rules, or if one is like that statistically negligible drunk driver who crosses the median strip; what if there's a rogue moray eel, victim of some terrible virus affecting the central nervous system, its genetically coded survival behavior, its good judgment; or some delinquent moray into gratuitous violence, a moray which just yearns to bite the poor mainland *haole* (foreign, hence white) "visitor," to reach up for a shot at his . . . manhood? Not to worry, I remind myself: I have moray eel T-shirts, have made the moray my totem animal, now promise to stop eating *unagi sushi.*

Not to worry:

> ". . . the sea, where every maw / The greater on the less feeds evermore . . ."
>
> —JOHN KEATS,
> Letter to Reynolds

And,

> "When you paddle out, you enter the food chain."
> —DR. SCOTT JENKINS

Still, not to worry: the opening of the film *Jaws,* legs dangling, dangling, as the camera stalks.

But in the ocean, in the ocean several saddleback wrasses (*hīnālea lau-wili*) go by. Talk about the mutable! If a supermale (bigger and more brightly colored than males from birth) dies, the largest female in the harem becomes one, assumes its role.

A large ray slowly flaps its wings, glides off into the underwater distance, into the murk and then the darkness, beyond the capacity of my eyes to see clearly, to see at all. "Oh, don't go," I hear myself muttering, feeling regret, loss.

Night approaches. Time, off shore, beyond the reef, for the approach of the "deep scattering layer," the vast, nearly world-wide nocturnal rising of enormous masses of deep-sea fish, shrimp, and squid, this migration of creatures surfacing in order to feed on plankton until descending again before dawn (something like 90 percent of all life on earth is in the water, they say). Meanwhile, day waning, I head in just after sunset, occasion near shore for a changing of the fish guard, nighttime hunters emerging, parrotfish building their nocturnal mucus cocoons, fish of all kinds losing their color. Because of the fading light, of course. But then it turns out to be also true that many fish do in fact change colors at night. Without my even being able to see them: minds, destinies, of their own.

ABLUTION. WASHING. PURIFYING. Cleaning. Cleansing. These different functions of water. Rinsing, laundering, bathing, douching. "In water," Eliade writes, "everything is 'dissolved' . . . everything that has happened ceases to exist . . . Immersion is the equivalent, at the human level, of death at the cosmic level, of the cataclysm (the Flood) which periodically dissolves the world into the primeval ocean. Breaking up all forms, doing away with the past, water possesses this power . . . of giving new birth." And, he argues, immersion "signifies regression to the preformal, reincorporation into the undifferentiated mode of pre-existence."

The problem now, Ivan Illich writes, is that water has lost its spiritual power, has been transformed into a cleaning fluid with chemical additives, an industrial detergent. Water "purification," water "treatment." Aeration, coagulation, sedimentation, filtration, disinfection, etc. Coagulants include alum, sodium aluminate, ferrous sulfate with lime, chlorinated copperas, ferric chloride, and ferric sulfate, all to reduce bacteria content or, indirectly, certain colors and tastes. Lime and soda ash are used to "soften" the water by removing calcium and magnesium. Chlorine is a disinfectant, as are ozone and ultraviolet radiation treatments; copper sulfate is for algae control. Think also of the use of fluoride to solve a nonlethal social problem, that is, dental decay caused by consumption of too much sugar. Opponents of fluoridation once called it a Communist conspiracy, but in any case fluoridation has nothing to do with water "purification." Consider also the 1960s counterculture fantasy of "turning on" the whole country by adding LSD—odorless, colorless, taste-less—to the water supply.

Man's ever-increasing domination of water: cisterns, wells, fountains, water wheels, norias, water screws, aqueducts, irriga-tion ditches, channels, drains, canals, sewers, dams, pipes, taps, hydrants, water towers, swimming pools, showers, baths, sinks. And the toilet, its water already repugnant to us. Not potable, we think: on its way to being sewage. Standing water, but not to be touched, there to absolve us from sight or smell of an aspect of our physical nature.

Man's domination of water. Archimedes, in the third century before Christ. The Archimedes screw, a circular pipe enclosing a helix, still in use in Egypt. And Archimedes *On Floating Bodies*. There is the story that King Hieron of Syracuse asked whether a crown made for him in fact contained only gold. In the bath one day, seeing the water overflowing, Archimedes realized that, if the crown were pure gold, it would displace an amount of water equal to that displaced by a piece of gold of the same weight; if alloyed with silver, which weighs less per volume than gold, the crown would displace a greater amount of water.

Man's hunger to master water. Leonardo Da Vinci defining his task for himself: "describe why water moves, and why its motion ceases; then why it becomes slower or more rapid; besides this, how it always falls . . . And how water rises in the air by means of the heat of the sun, and then falls again in rain; why water springs forth from the tops of mountains."

Though Ivan Illich may be right, though humans have transformed water into a chemical detergent—not to mention "acid rain," that almost oxymoron—still it is held to possess spiritual powers. Hindu pilgrims in the Ganges, of course; Christians being baptized. And observant Jews in the *mikvah*, the ritual bath, part of the water of which cannot be drawn through human intervention (hence the use of rainwater in most *mikvahs*). As Areyeh Kaplan explains, the Talmud says the source of all water is the river in Eden, to which Jews can reestablish their link in the *mikvah*. Immersion in this water changes spiritual status, is not a cleansing but a purification. More, Kaplan writes, "water is the essence of impermanence," has the power to nullify the self. Thus, "When a person enters the *mikvah*, he subjugates his ego to God." Finally, the *mikvah* represents both womb and grave. In immersion, the individual momentarily enters the realm of the nonliving. Emerging as if resurrected; as if born again.

> "I once knew a writer who, after saying beautiful things about the sea, passed through a Pacific hurricane, and he became a changed man."
> —Joshua Slocum,
> *Sailing Alone Around the World*

G LASSY, THAT STATE OF GRACE: no wind, no noise, board shooting along, waves perfectly defined, absolutely themselves, their shape not affected by any other force, a realm of clarity and ease. Water thick as milk, as cream. As porridge.

A windless winter day, after a month of cold. Very heavy rain, each drop making a small crater on the ocean surface, but despite the cumulative impact of so many minute explosions the net effect is to calm the water, to eliminate all other normal movement or pattern—ripple, chip, groove, rill. In the torrential downpour, each successive incoming wave seems smooth, sheer, immaculate, pure as the formula of the textbook curve.

Poet Philip Larkin: "If I were called in / To construct a

religion / I should make use of water." Not to think of believing in the Almighty or not believing in the Almighty one way or the other, but then to hear the words on one's lips after two hours in the surf: "Thank you, God."

For what? Oh, for this pulsing, undulating, shimmering, sighing, breathing plasma of an ocean. For the miracle of warm water. For rideable waves and no wind.

"However, if sail you must, take my advice: never trust all you possess on board of a ship. Leave the greater part at home, and freight your vessels with the lesser part only. For I say again it's a terrible thing to perish at sea."

—HESIOD,
Works and Days

At twenty-two, I got what I asked for, a chance to go cruising on a sailing vessel. In this case, a forty-foot trimaran built and skippered by a man taking it south to sell in the wake of his divorce. The Ur prenautical saga: couple separates after years of building a boat weekends and holidays, planning a voyage to the South Seas. (Noah's wife declines to come aboard.) Not a happy occasion for the skipper, therefore, but for me, oh, the world was my oyster as we headed out of Sausalito under the Golden Gate.

We sailed west-southwest seven miles or so, then made a left turn. Nothing to be seen in any direction except ocean, more ocean. At which point I began to feel sick, very sick. It wasn't the motion of the boat—trimarans are inspired by traditional Polynesian outriggers, have no heavy keel to counterbalance the sail, are light by comparison with western monohulls, far more in tune with the swell, can surf, adding wave speed to wind speed. No, it wasn't the motion of the boat, or even the endlessly rising and falling horizon line. Rather, it was that I suddenly understood we were very far out to sea, that I could not handle the boat alone should anything happen to the skipper—and he was clearly quite depressed, down below working on a glass of whiskey. There at the helm, keeping the course he'd set, I knew we were less than a matchstick, not even a cork bobbing on that vastness where whales would be nothing in the vastness, on the relentless upwelling we were so smoothly riding. Sails taut, vessel accelerating and then slowing over and over again as we'd gain and then lose the surge below us, I vowed that if I somehow made it safe to shore, if I just made it home, I'd never, ever go to sea again.

But of course I did end up with my own sailing vessel. Ghosting in across San Francisco Bay at sunset, Jupiter and Venus just above the horizon, Sutro tower like a gigantic tuning fork over the city, grebes, coots, herons, murres, and pterodactyllic pelicans for companions, as well as the occasional huge honeybee landing on deck. Or under full sail in high winds below the Golden Gate Bridge, boat driving hard, making not an iota of headway against the current. Or: rust remover, acetone, resin, putty. Hauling the boat out, up an ancient and rickety marine railway on the Oakland Estuary, to spend weeks scraping and painting the hull, drowning in keeping the boat afloat, losing track of my life until it was no longer clear whether I was a writer with a boat or a boat repairman who also thought of doing some writing. Spending money like . . . a sailor!

Pouring dollars into that floating hole for yet another piece of "essential" gear, experiencing the anxieties a boat inevitably bestows, becoming the martinet a boat sometimes requires, these aspects of sustaining life on an element not one's own.

WATCHING WATER. Clouds: In Genesis God separated "the waters from the waters"; clouds/vapor/rain are the water above the firmament. According to Louis Ginzberg, "On the second day of creation, the waters rebelled against this separation. . . . The waters destined to be up high refused to leave the embrace of the waters resting below, and they embraced each other more closely . . . weeping . . ."

Clouds: water vapor in air condensing into minute drops because of falling temperature. Part of the miraculous yet daily cycle of evaporation and precipitation enabling the life of the planet, this process of heat absorption and release providing the requisite thermal stability. Extraordinary, the role of the sun in transmuting water, occasioning its metamorphosis, distilling it, ridding it of impurities, even converting salt water to fresh. Extraordinary, the role of the sun, but hardly obvious. Aristotle, for instance, believed a subterranean fire heated the ocean, whose waters thus formed reservoirs which in turn fed rivers. Not until the eighteenth century did Halley hypothesize the atmospheric cycle of water. Now the cycle has become quantifiable, but the vocabularies of physics, metereology, and hydrology that describe our reading of water sometimes obscure or diminish what is most miraculous. As Christophe Girot points out, it is still true, as it was in the Middle Ages, that water "is the alchemical mediator between fire and earth." Sunset over the ocean, in any case: clouds giving would-be artists yet another course in perspective.

Watching water: Toward ten P.M. Just past full moon behind us over the Ko'olaus, rain clouds coming around the corner of Diamond Head in front of us as we sit on the seawall, palms swaying, surge breaking, waves black with white foam. Suddenly, an enormous lunar bow materializes—fluorescent green, almost phosphorescent. Makes itself known, comes into our ken, arching down from the rain clouds toward the horizon, slowly widening on the left to include red and orange tones.

Time stops, as if such beauty is in no hurry to move with more than serenity; one feels a strange calm, gratitude for the privilege of being a witness. And then the bow is gone, leaving an effort to retain what the eye saw, a yearning for what is already beyond telling.

Full fathom five thy father lies;
Of his bones are coral made;
Those are pearls that were his eyes:
Nothing of him that doth fade,
But doth suffer a sea change
Into something rich and strange.
                    —SHAKESPEARE, *The Tempest*

WATER IS A KIND OF DESTINY," Gaston Bachelard wrote. "A being dedicated to water is a being in flux . . . Water always flows, always falls, always ends in horizontal death . . . death associated with water is more dream-like than death associated with earth: the pain of water is infinite."

From the Honolulu morning paper:

> An inexperienced surfer who paddled out into eight-to
> 10-foot surf at Sandy Beach yesterday had to be rescued
> by the Fire Department helicopter after he was caught in
> the rip current . . . a lifeguard noticed the 21-year-old

surfer being swept toward Hanauma at about 4:50 P.M., and tried to swim out to help him.

When that failed, the lifeguard returned to get a bodyboard and reached the surfer as the current took him just outside the surf breaking on the rocks near the Blowhole . . .

The two paddled back toward Sandy Beach, but the surfer refused to go back through the shorebreak, so the helicopter picked them up at 5:25 P.M. . . .

The raging main. The fear not injury but death by drowning. "Those are pearls that were his eyes." Immersions/baptisms/transformations/cleansings/dissolutions. A "sea change into something rich and strange." Notable local drownings: Hawaiian activists George Helm and Kimo Mitchell (their surfboard found thirteen miles off the island of Lāna'i); waterman Eddie Aikau; waterman Jose Angel. All lost at sea. Lost at sea. ("I go down with the guys who are out," says surfer Charlie Walker in Jenkins's *North Shore Chronicles.* "I go down with Eddie [Aikau]—every time I go out, I see him. I see life, I see death. I see every mistake I've made.") Poet Stevie Smith: "I was not waving but drowning." Surfer Fred Van Dyke: "I was held down . . . I'd swim frantically up ten feet, see light, but then get sucked back down again."

But also, being in the water as counterphobic. Buzzy Trent: "Waves are not measured in feet or inches, they are measured in increments of fear." Of Greg Noll—"Da Bull"—at Mākaha in 1969, Fred Hemmings testifies, in Noll's memoir: "All of us were on shore as he finally stroked into a wave that filled the whole horizon . . . It was a death-wish wave. He elevator-dropped to the bottom. The wave broke over him. . . . I think he was glad to be alive. I *know* he was lucky to be alive." On the beach, Noll's friend Buffalo Keaulana greeted him with a beer.

" 'Good ting you men make 'em, Brudda,' " Keaulana said. " 'Cause no way I was comin' in afta you. I was jus goin' wave goodbye and say 'Alooo-ha.' " Though this day has become story—the biggest wave ever attempted?—Noll's wife writes that it was quite a while before her husband—who seemed always to enjoy the wipeouts as much as the rides, who would laugh underwater, pinned down at the bottom, waiting for the wave to release him—would speak of that day at all. (It is perhaps not surprising that having tested this limit—and survived—Noll subsequently made a decision to give up surfing altogether.)

Poet Gerard Manley Hopkins, his "widow-making unchilding unfathering/deeps." Nearly everyone, it seems, once nearly drowned, can shudder to remember, has a story to tell. Like Steve the architect, whose mother was bathing him when he was an infant but then fainted and fell down on him and they both nearly drowned. This saga recounted to his future wife, Bo, after she'd prepared to seduce him soon after they first met. Apparently Bo left a note on the front door telling Steve to come on in, meanwhile arraying herself in a bubble bath to surprise and encourage him. Calling her name, looking for her in the apartment, Steve finally made it as far as the bathroom door. Was able to tell Bo the story only after he recovered from having fainted at the sight of her. (And, after they married, would participate in an updated version of the tale.)

Near drownings. Well on in *Moby Dick*, Pip, the little black sailor, replaces an injured man in Stubbs' whaleboat. Pip's first outing, nothing untoward happens, but the next time, startled just after the whale is harpooned, Pip leaps overboard and is nearly strangled by the line as the whale begins to run. To save Pip, Stubb has the line cut, and the whale is lost. " 'Stick to the boat,' " Stubb warns, "or by the Lord, I won't pick you up.' "

Their next time out, however, Pip again leaps overboard, so Stubb leaves Pip behind "like a hurried traveller's trunk . . . It was a beautiful, bounteous, blue day; the spangled sea calm and cool, and flatly stretching away, all round, to the horizon . . .

"Now, in calm weather, to swim in the open ocean is as easy to the practiced swimmer as to ride in a spring-carriage ashore. But the awful lonesomeness is intolerable. The intense concentration of self in the middle of such a heartless immensity, my God! who can tell it?"

Stubb had supposed the whaleboats behind him would pick Pip up, but as it happened they too gave chase to whales. It was only by accident, then, that the *Pequod* itself later rescued him, but by then Pip was "an idiot; such, at least, they said he was. The sea had jeeringly kept his finite body up, but drowned the infinite of his soul. Not drowned entirely, though. Rather carried down alive to wondrous depths, where strange shapes of the unwarped primal world glided to and fro before his passive eyes; and the miser-merman, Wisdom, revealed his hoarded heaps; and among the joyous, heartless, ever-juvenile eternities, Pip saw the multitudinous, God-omnipresent, coral insects, that out of the firmament of waters heaved the colossal orbs. He saw God's foot upon the treadle of the loom, and spoke it; and therefore his shipmates called him mad." Crazed with wisdom, Pip had achieved a true dispassion about human "weal or woe," was now as "uncompromised, indifferent as his God."

The fear of drowning. "Now would I give a thousand furlongs of sea for an acre of barren ground; long heath, brown furze, any thing," says Gonzalo in *The Tempest*. "The wills above be done! but I would fain die a dry death." Years and years ago, children on the shore of a cold and clear New England lake, we learned to swim, as had generations before us, by practicing the "dead man's float." An early hint, perhaps, a sign for the very young, that from humans water would require not only mastery but surrender.

FOUR P.M. Monday through Friday, off the sea ladder, about fifteen yards from shore. The same group of five or six or seven senior citizens, floating, gossiping. Out past them toward the reef, the same old man who's well offshore every day, doing his very slow, achingly slow backstroke, riding high in the water like some kind of marine mammal. Coming from? Going to?

Seeing him pass; waiting for waves at Tongg's during a long lull. One ponders, dreams. Waves: horizontally mobile transient vortexes. Lions in the wild, sometimes. A kind of ecstasy simply to be in the presence of such truth, such majesty . . . such capacity to inspire terror.

Waiting, still, when a long, thin, red board shoots past, sharp as a stiletto, surfer paddling with authority, purpose, knowledge, power. Heading out, out, south—south toward Antarctica!—with such desire that one has no choice but to follow.

According to Herodotus, when a bridge over the Hellespont broke, Xerxes commanded that the Hellespont be whipped with a scourge and that a pair of fetters be let down into the sea. "I have, moreover, heard that with them he likewise sent branding instruments to brand the Hellespont." And there is the Persian emperor Cyrus, who, after the drowning of one of his sacred white horses some twenty-four hundred years ago, disciplined the river Gyndus by having it divided into 360 channels.

Foolish Xerxes? Vain Cyrus? Consider the Aswan Dam, silt building up behind it at a prodigious rate, schistosomiasis increasing down below. Or consider Psalm 77: "When the waters saw thee, O God, when the waters saw thee, they were afraid, yea, the deep trembled."

Contagious, such a frame of mind: some surfers out there relentlessly chastening the waves.

WATER, according to Guy Motil, is "opaque, transparent, reflective, or a combination of all these." As light enters water, various parts of the visible spectrum are affected differently. The longer, red wavelengths are quickly filtered out —absorbed—in shallow water, converted into heat, shorter wavelengths absorbed only in deeper water (though even blue light, which penetrates most easily, reaches a depth of no more than one thousand meters). Also, David Doubilet writes, sunlight is transformed when it enters the sea; in the deep blue, other colors change. "Red becomes black, blue veins look green. Some yellows become mustardy, others stay bright." (A photographer's underwater flash supposedly "like" or "contains" the values of sunlight, thus "restoring" the surface spectrum, which of course doesn't exist here, thus allowing images on film that the human eye in water cannot see. Cannot see, that is, even from inside a mask, since the human eye, adapted for air, loses its focusing power in water.)

Consider, then, the depth of the vast lake of the Pacific off the Kona Coast of the Big Island of Hawai'i. Deep water, bluer than longing. And, in the vast wind shadow of Mauna Loa (nearly fourteen thousand feet above sea level, running down to a base more than twelve thousand feet below sea level), the surface startlingly calm, flat, silent. Below this liquid mirror, *aqua incognita*, a filled but empty space except for countless tiny plankton, just visible transparent microplanets. All quite unlike the teeming primal soup of the reef with its variety of colors/shapes/strategies/urgencies, what Ted Mooney called "the sea's blunt fecundity." In this deep blue, all alone, one as if inevitably begins to catalogue its qualities, to search for appropriate prepositions, verbs, nouns. All right, one is *in* it. *Surrounded* by it? *Engulfed* by it? Or, yes, it's *transparent*, but of course one's visiblity is quite limited. Or is this blue a *void*? Can something be nothing? Or, what's the *scale*, anyway? No help there: no referents in no matter what direction. But if not scale, what of *vector*? The plankton, for example: *floating? dropping? (held) in suspension?* All these questions unanswered as enormous broad shafts of light spiral . . . *up from down under*, as if somewhere below a gala film opening is being celebrated. Remake of *Alice's Adventures in Wonderland*, perhaps.

Back to the surface for air, up through the quicksilver interface, having overcome the quite palpable tug from below, and . . . there's life. Dorsal fins approaching: as if to confuse things further, the play of dolphins, the endless circling wheel of their surfacing and diving. And here they are, more or less: squadrons, armadas, flotillas, echelons, convoys, holding just below in formation, in a display of skill, the Blue Angels of the deep blue. "Check this out," they seem to be saying, exhibitionists of this liquid Sahara. Forget the spinning, individual dolphins over and again surging up through the surface as if for a toke of gravity, try these group routines to make you ooo and ahhh like the dancing of the Rockettes at Rockefeller Center. So you look: There they are, perhaps thirteen of them, one/four/two/four/two, front to back. But even as your eye sees this, the formation alters both depth and angle, though without visible movement, so that as the image is perceived it is already in jeopardy or is in fact lost. Another image taking its place at a different distance, or perhaps now the formation has also changed, is now one lead dolphin and a football-shaped cluster behind. Student body left. Even the MTV-trained eye beginning to rebel against such transitions. At which point, click, a small pod is within touching distance, dolphins angling, right eyes staring, one's own eye now staring at the cookie cutter shark bites, which seem enormous even as one reminds oneself: *water magnifies.* Further confusing the eye-mind dialogue. The dolphins then not suddenly but suddenly, that is, without apparent use of any force, both simultaneously alongside and heading away, spiraling down in one of those primary patterns, the formula governing growth of the chambered nautilis/proportions of the human body/patterns of leaf growth/efficiency of projectiles in air.

At which point, click/click, spiral dissolves, squadron again holding just below and . . . shitting. Now what, you might ask, what's the message? Choose one:

    a. It is normal for dolphins to shit; they think nothing of it, nor should we.
    b. Dolphins shit in front of others only rarely; this is a great honor; in fact, one should reciprocate.
    c. Though twenty to forty feet below, the dolphins are shitting on one, so to speak.
    (Dolphin feces may contain sexual pheromones or other chemical traces, which would explain why they seem at times to intentionally make passes through their school's field of excrement. Or: such passes may simply be some kind of a game, etc.)

Oops, now flukes are moving, dolphins having in a moment shifted planes, down and away into what is both transparent and invisible. *Gone,* by God. There only the moment before, but, from the very start of contact, threatening to move beyond one's capacity to apprehend them. Their very presence, constantly intimating the boundary of perception, having induced ongoing visual confusion—focus! focus!—as well as a form of despair at the nonstop effort to retain an image of them on the retina.

Alone in the endless blue, one searches for something to cling to. Data, for instance: What species were they? "No problem," comes the answer from the deep: "Imagine, say, *Balinese* dolphins." Which is to suggest, not just play, but shadow play.

(As for the apparent difficulty of the human eye in taking in the immediate presence of dolphins, the unsettling sensation that the dolphins must be using their sonar to disrupt one's capacity to see or remember, this is no accident. According to Kenneth Norris, if a "dolphin is among enough others that look very much like it, if all face the same general direction and move in generally the same way," then attacks by large predators will fail. Part of this has to do with the incapacity of a vertebrate's eye to track more than six or eight objects at any given moment, part to do with the extraordinary coordination of the dolphin school, which can outmaneuver attackers even as it denies them any coherent point of reference.)

T WO SHIPS PASSING in the night. Water seeks its own level. Blood's thicker than water. Hold your water. Bodies of water. Still waters run deep. In over your head. Unfathomable. High and dry. Landlocked. To feel drained. To go with the flow. An outpouring of emotion. To sense that one is stagnating. A free flow of ideas. Circulating a memo. Washed out. Get my drift? That's water over the dam.

Flotsam: "Such part of the wreckage of a ship and its cargo as is found floating on the water. Hence, anything floating or drifting about on, or as on, the surface of a body of water." *Jetsam:* "Goods thrown overboard to lighten a vessel in distress . . . (var. of jetson, syncopated form of jettison; final m as in flotsam, etc.)" *Jettison:* "Act of casting overboard (. . . var. of getaison, der. geter throw)." *Flotsam and jetsam:* "The wreckage of a ship and its cargo found either floating upon the sea or washed ashore; odds and ends."

Flotsam and jetsam: words from the realm of the sea that contain an oddly disturbing power when extended to dry land. For instance: *human* flotsam and jetsam. A terrible fate implied, to be as on the water in this way. In the form of at least partial consolation, however, we should also remember *lagan:* "Goods sunk in the sea with a buoy attached in order that they may be found again."

French: *La mer,* the sea (fem.). *L'océan,* the ocean (masc.). *L'eau,* water (fem.). *Le fleuve,* the river (masc.). German: *Das Meer* (neut.); *die See* (fem.). [And *der See* (masc.) = lake.] *Der Ozean* (masc.). *Das Wasser* (neut.). *Der Fluss* (masc.) Die Nordsee: the North sea, which is also called Die Mordsee, the Murder Sea. Hebrew and Arabic: sea, water, and river: masc. Icelandic: water and ocean, neut.; sea and river, fem. Chinese: nouns have no gender, but see the distinction between Yin and Yang. Yin: moist, fertile, receptive, female. Yang: dry, fertilizing, male.

In Hemingway's *Old Man and the Sea,* "He always thought of the sea as *la mar* which is what people call her in Spanish when they love her. Sometimes those who love her say bad things of her but they are always said as though she were a woman. Some of the younger fishermen . . . spoke of her as *el mar* which is masculine . . . as a contestant or a place or even an enemy. But the old man always thought of her as feminine and as something that gave or withheld great favors, and if she did wild or wicked things it was because she could not help them. The moon affects her as it does a woman, he thought." (According to Erich Neumann in *The Great Mother,* "Since water is undifferentiated and elementary and is often uroboric, containing male elements side by side with the maternal, flowing and moving waters, such as streams, are bisexual and male and are worshipped as fructifiers and movers.")

Beyond these forms of conceptualizing water in language, language itself, Bachelard argues, "has a *liquid quality,* a flow in its overall effect, water in its consonants." Not that this comes as a surprise to him: "Streams and rivers *provide the sound* for mute country landscapes . . . murmuring waters teach birds and men to sing, speak, recount . . . there is, in short, a continuity between the speech of water and speech of man." (N.B: Avoid babbling brooks.)

Put another way in an (imaginary?) text quoted in A. S. Byatt's *Possession*, a novel, "Such pleasure in the shapeless yet patterned succession of waters, in the formless yet formed sequence of waves on the shore, is essentially present in the art of Virginia Woolf and the form of her sentences, her utterance, themselves."

(California surf language of the sixties and seventies, with its understatement, irony, abbreviation: "How was?"; "Got wet"; "Pretty fun." "Shred and gnarl.")

"What are you staring at, mariner man
Wrinkled as sea-sand and old as the sea?"

—EDITH SITWELL

REACHING THE WATER AGAIN, one smiles. A smile of recognition, quick, a reflex flash. As when encountering a close friend again. Like a baby's smile, without apparent reference to externals perceived by adult eyes. To come back down to the ocean is to reexperience an essential memory trace, something once known well, to recall that one has been trying to remember.

Water music at Sandy Beach. Boomboxes in every pickup and van, vibration of the bass audible, palpable in the solar plexus, for hundreds of yards. Jawaiian music, Jamaican-Hawaiian, Rasta T-shirts popular here. All this as locals sit watching incoming waves—and the bodysurfers risking paralysis in the shore break—for hours at a time. As at a drive-in movie. As on the Fourth of July.

What's to show for all this watching . . . such fishing with nothing caught? John Keats urged those whose eyeballs are "vex'd and tired" to "Feast them upon the wideness of the Sea." Farmer/curmudgeon Robert Frost, however, chided those who thus "turn their back on the land":

> They cannot look out far.
> They cannot look in deep.
> But when was that ever a bar
> To any watch they keep?

Herman Melville, on the other hand, asked, "Were Niagara but a cataract of sand, would you travel your thousand miles to see it?" (Charles Darwin, a seasick sailor who had perhaps voyaged too long, wrote that though it "is well once to behold a squall with its rising arch and coming fury," a storm is in fact "an incomparably finer spectacle when beheld on shore, where the waving trees, the wild flight of the birds, the dark shadows and bright lights, the rushing of the torrents, all proclaim the strife of the unloosed elements. At sea the albatross and little petrel fly as if the storm were their proper sphere, the water rises and sinks as if fulfilling its usual task.")

As for reaching the ocean again after having been away, often one marvels that it was possible to be gone so long, ever to have left. "How did I get so far from water?" asks poet Elizabeth Bishop's Strayed Crab. And there is the response of those who, having struggled to reach the sea, finally achieve it. Keats' "stout Cortez" (Balboa, actually), who "with eagle eyes . . . star'd at the Pacific—and all his men / Look'd at each other with a wild surmise— / Silent, upon a peak in Darien." Or the experience of the Greek mercenaries after Cyrus failed in his attempt on the Persian throne. As Xenophon writes, pushing north, the Greeks fought their way toward home, their goal the Euxine Sea. One day, "as the vanguard got to the top of a mountain, a great shout went up. And when Xenophon and soldiers heard it, they imagined that other enemies were attacking in front. . . . But as the shout kept getting louder and nearer, as the successive ranks that came up all began to run at full speed toward the ranks ahead that were one after another joining in the shout, and as the shout kept growing and louder as the number of men grew steadily greater, it became quite clear to Xenophon that here was something of unusual importance; so he . . . pushed ahead to lend aid; and in a moment they heard the soldiers shouting, '*Thalassa! thalassa!* The sea, the sea!' "

"The corpses of men float face upward, those of women face down, as if nature wished to respect the modesty of dead women."

—Pliny the Elder

Drowning, the thing itself. Third leading cause of accidental deaths in the United States—5,400 in 1984, primarily children and young adults, most of them males—and an estimated 50,000 near-drownings annually. Given hot tubs, boating, and the popularity of water sports, experts believe half the population is at risk of drowning each year.

In a way, however, it's odd we are able to drown; babies, Watson argues, can swim "long before they ever learn to sit up or crawl. . . . paddling easily up to the surface whenever they need to breathe. They never ever try to do so with their heads underwater . . . [it is] only later that we lose these instincts . . . Which seems unnecessary, because . . . we are unique among land animals in that we have a 'dive reflex,' a marked reduction

THOMAS FARBER

in heart rate and oxygen consumption, which takes over automatically as soon as water touches our faces." (There are also those rudimentary webs between fingers and thumbs.) Further, we eat vegetables that are nearly entirely water, and we ourselves are as waterlogged as fish, two-thirds water—ten to fifteen gallons in most of us (human brains are three-quarters liquid, bones more than 20 percent liquid, the just-formed human fetus nearly entirely water). Also, it's true that we are hairless mammals, like dolphins and hippos—water creatures all. And that our bodies, like those of marine mammals, are insulated with subcutaneous fat, making us both buoyant and streamlined. And that, like dolphins, we can produce a variety of nasal sounds, perhaps a function of the breath control diving requires. (In Europe, various doctors, believing that newborns are aquatic creatures and that the transition from womb to world includes a powerful shock of gravity, have apparently been birthing babies in water tanks in hospitals. One, it seems, has also delivered babies in the Black Sea, with a pod of dolphins nearby to telepathically instill their intelligence in the babies.)

Nonetheless: You can drown in a tablespoon of water. Some people panic as they inhale that first quantity of liquid, which causes the larynx to go into violent spasms—laryngospasm. Though there's no water in the lungs, or very little, they axphyxiate, die because of the lack of oxygen. It happens to babies and to those who in the water are seized by fear. Such drowning is called "dry drowning," and occurs in something like 15 percent of all cases.

The second kind of drowning, including taking in a larger quantity of water, is often more gradual. You are out in the ocean, for example. You get water in your lungs. Humans need oxygen, get rid of CO_2. If we can't, the acid in the body increases, and as it does you get sleepy. Just before you become unconscious, besides the burning feeling of suffocation, there may be delirium because the brain begins to swell. You may feel a wave of relief, a sense of return to the amniotic. ("I almost drowned," a doctor recalls. "I felt, finally, that life is a struggle but that death would be easy. When I saw a boat coming to save me, I felt dejected because I was being pulled back into the maelstrom that was life.")

Also, drownings in fresh and saltwater are not the same. The chemical composition of blood is similar to that of saltwater, so if your lungs fill up with saltwater you can aspirate—breathe— more of it than you can fresh water. When you drown in saltwater, you suffocate because oxygen can't get across the square miles of membrane that are our lungs. But if you have saltwater—that is, blood—on one side of those membranes and fresh water on the other, the effort to balance the electrolytes (potassium, sodium, chloride) deranges your blood, changes the blood chemistry. There is still oxygen across the lungs, but you die because salt is leaking out of the blood and into the water you swallowed. Your heart starts to fibrillate and then stops. Speaking of the spirit, a prisoner in Alexander Solzhenitsyn's novel *The First Circle* remarks that it is better to drown in the ocean than in the puddle. Given the physiology involved, it appears that the prisoner could have been speaking of the body as well.

(Much of this medical knowledge has been gained from studies with laboratory animals—rats and dogs. Increasing humanity's knowledge of drowning through animal experimentation is not, it seems, for the weak of heart.)

Four-year-old Hsu Li, uneasy about being in the tub when the plug is pulled—the danger of spiraling down and out with all that water. And, reassured that there can be no dangerous fish—that is, sharks—in the swimming pool because it is not saltwater, he asks, "But why don't they put in salt?" (An interesting question. They could add salt, but then it still would not be seawater. The ocean has had much the same composition for several billion years, but the salts of the sea could be accumulated in only a few million years of runoff from land. That is, the salts of seawater represent a balance or equilibrium: materials constantly added and removed. Further, seawater cannot be duplicated in a laboratory because it is not merely water plus salt but an ecosystem containing millions of organisms. Millions of microviruses, that is to say, in a single teaspoon of seawater: most of the biomass in the ocean, and most of the energy flow, is of and by organisms too small to see. As Marston Bates points out, when you take seawater home from the beach, the water itself seems to decay: "It is hard to avoid the impression . . . that seawater is a mysterious, magical substance." (As for the danger of going down the drain, consider Slothrop's voyage down the toilet and through the sewers of Boston in Thomas Pynchon's *Gravity's Rainbow*.)

Hsu Li at seven and a half: Child of his times; child of his age. Tongue curled, sticking out à la Michael Jordan. Teeth being lost all the time, tooth fairy making frequent visits (faith at this stage sustained by tangible under-the-pillow benefits). Hsu Li masticating five sticks of gum, cheek chipmunked like a major leaguer's, poring over the box scores in the morning sports page as if proper study of the stats promises revelation of deeper meanings. Nonetheless, not a die-hard fan, in fact unable to sit watching a game for very long. Enthusiastic, but in the moment itself not much concerned with outcome.

Hsu Li luxuriating in his bath, in no hurry at all. Out, drying desultorily, towel then dropped on the floor, and back to his room to again rearrange his seven hundred—plus baseball cards, or laughing with surprise as he farts: mysterious, always, the body, but no source of dismay. "Excuse me," he says, grinning.

Hsu Li and diet. A sugar freak, yes, but also a fruit and vegetable palate, meat still something like an acquired taste. A new period of neotony, legs and torso elongating once again. No body fat, ribs right there to be counted. Boni Moroni . . .

And with what thoughts in the young male mind? Heroic fantasies matched with a very short attention span. Not flushing the toilet, for instance, but no visible malice in this, just a whole other movie in the brain by the time the underpants are pulled up. As for ritual cleansing . . .

"Did you wash your hands?"

"Yes."

"Really?"

"Yes."

"But the soap is as dry as bone in there."

"Oh."

As for what the mental computer contains, data being accumulated at a prodigious rate: "Last one in's a rotten egg. First is the worst, second is the best, third is the one with the polka dot dress." Or, "Last one in is a rotten egg, everyone included, no talk backs." Or, "I was walking down the hall / scratching my balls / When my balls got stuck in the elevator walls. / My balls turned green / My mother screamed / And that was the end of my ding-a-ling-a-ling." All this in synch with strangely precise fragments of memory, something someone mentioned at a party when he was four, or the length and weight of the blue whale. This and a dazzling capacity to arrive somewhat to the side of the point. For instance, learning about an environmental activist who, working as a crewman on a tuna fishing vessel, took the risk of making videotapes of dolphins being slaughtered, and hearing that copies of the film were then sent around to TV stations, Hsu Li interrupts to ask, "How many copies?"

Hsu Li at seven and a half, more lover than fighter, perhaps because he is adequately loved, possessed of an occasional sweet, reflective smile, as if lost for a moment in the savor of some small wonder. And, now, on vacation, back for another extended stay at the ocean. Immediately into the water for hours at a time. Oh, the joy of gear: boogie board; black XCEL vest against board rash and wind chill; goggles for body surfing. The learning curve of beginning to ride waves. Getting the board balanced side to side. Then the issue of weight end to end: too far forward, you fall down the face of the wave; too far back, you miss it. In a way, the course of Hsu Li's exploration of the form's possibilities seems inevitable, a recapitulation of what the species has achieved. With surf-riding vehicles as with, say, the guitar: once you have six strings tuned E-A-D, etc., the blues inevitably emerge. Techno-determinism, Hsu Li thus willy milly on his way to el rollos and 360's.

Motive, however, is a mystery; he appears to have arrived not determined to learn—there's no sense of intention, really—but as though it's a given, that the surf will be his focus. Surely there's joy being on the waves, a hunger for mastery, the desire to do what other kids can do, the need to please significant others, though all this must be measured against the obvious danger, appropriate fear. But perhaps Hsu Li simply intuits that such an equation, plus and minus, is about as good as we get. Whatever the reasons, though six months ago still wary of the deep end of a pool, now he's in that classic pose, head up, blessedly flexible back in something close to the Salute to the Sun posture in Yoga, searching for what's on the horizon, scanning the waves as he floats like a leaf, like a water spider. And no sooner has he learned to read and catch waves—getting positioned and steeling himself against the all-too-human impulse to pull back—then he's trying to kneel on the board, trying to stand.

High tide, waves looking good, and Hsu Li overcomes prudence to take a very large drop, or perhaps it was inadvertent, but there he is, shrieking as he hurtles down the face, is millraced toward shore, now shouting "Bail, bail," before acting on his own exhortations, abandoning the board just before it accelerates into the seawall. Then reclaiming the board, flopping down to ride the backwash out—repetition compulsion of the worst kind—until he's again being chased by the whitewater, legs flying, or arriving on shore triumphant, fingers in V for victory, finally getting to his feet as if to prove that he still can, or to pause to appraise what might have been had things not gone so well, talking to himself nonstop, doing his own play by play, cathartic consolation, or celebration. Or there's a break for some quasi-karate, challenging incoming waves with punches and kicks, force against force, at last a fair fight.

Sunset itself, which doesn't much interest him—too deliberate an event? In the long afterglow, Hsu Li still at it, intoxicated perhaps by the endlessly shifting levels as he rides the swell waiting for a set, one minute well above a friend only several feet away, one minute well below. Light waning, waning until he can barely make out the wave as it begins to form.

Supper, teeth to be brushed. A very humid night, no trades, Hsu Li down, fast, and sleeping without a cover, teddy bear nearby, much to process, absorb, incorporate, to organize, to render safe. As the poet wrote, "Dream is dark, dream is deep, I swim an ocean in my sleep."

S EA STORIES that hold our attention: Jonah's, for instance— or Noah's. You remember, "The Lord saw that the wickedness of man was great in the earth, and that every imagination of the thoughts of his heart was only evil continually. And the Lord was sorry that he had made man on the earth, and it grieved him to His heart. So the Lord said, 'I will blot out man whom I have created from the face of the ground, man and beast and creeping things and birds of the air, for I am sorry that I have made them." And so He did blot them out, "everything on the dry land in whose nostrils was the breath of life," all except for the righteous six hundred–year-old Noah and his family and the animals aboard the ark. (Though we term this the flood, the deluge came from below and above: "On that day all the foundations of the great deep burst forth, and the windows on the heavens were opened." God, it seems, was undoing his original parting of the waters.) You'll remember also that, after the rains stopped and the waters were dried up, God gave Noah the rainbow sign, the sign of water and light combined, a convenant with Noah and his descendants that the waters would never again "destroy all flesh."

My mother was deeply drawn to the Noah story, as a writer

came back to it again and again. In *Did You Know It Was the Narwhale?*, she asked,

> Did you know it was the Unicorn,
> bounding through the wood,
> who rounded up the animals by twos,
> male and female,
> and led them to the landing where old Noah stood,
> checking an alphabetical reservation list . . .

The Unicorn continued to help Noah, and finally cast off the lines as the ark departed. But now there was no more room on board, and of course the Unicorn was one of a kind, only pairs allowed. Nonetheless, appreciating so much help, Noah offered to tow the Unicorn behind, and of course it could then assist with disembarking—when and if they arrived. But as my mother asked:

> Did you know that forty days can seem forever if
>   you're floating
> in the wake of an overloaded Ark?
> And forty nights forever multiplied?
> The Unicorn grew wretched in all that dampness,
> all those waters . . .

> Did you know the woods had long since drowned
> within his weary watery memory,
> deep as ever they perished under the flood?
> His hooves could pound no springing earth.
> His nose could smell no fragrant, trampled balsam
>   needles.
> His mouth tasted no tart young shoots.
> He rested in no shadows
> where a friendly sun played hide-and-seek.
> The waves, slap-slapping, scuttled the last leaf-rustle
> out of his ears.

It was only when a white Beluga whale—"The smallest whale," seven-and-a-half-year-old Hsu Li explains as we read the story—came by on the morning of the fortieth day and called him cousin that the flabbergasted Unicorn suddenly realized that shank, knee, and hoof were gone, that with flippers and a different kind of tail it had become . . . well of course! A Narwhale.

Subsequently, in *Where's Gomer*, with illustrations by William Pene du Bois, my mother imagined Noah's grandson late for the ark. At last, minus one small boy, "in the storm and the cold and the waves and wet," the ark departs:

> O tempest and flood! O watery ways
> of dismal darks and desolate grays!
> O deluge! O umpteen nights and days
>   without Gomer!

But again, the landfall at Ararat is not the only miracle: there, stepping ashore from the back of a dolphin, is . . . Gomer!

Finally, in *How the Left-Behind Beasts Built Ararat*, with woodcuts by Antonio Frasconi, my mother took up the great question that has for so long tormented Talmudic scholars: why did the innocent animals perish in the flood? If for Noah there must have been the fear that the rains wouldn't come, sons and daughters and grandchildren restless there in the dust of the camp on shore, bickering, bickering, perhaps his greater worry was why the Lord his God had to make a desert to justify a flood.

> Noah was sorry. Noah was kind.
> He hoped the beasts wouldn't terribly mind
> that he had to be leaving so many behind
> in the wind and the cold, the mud, the rain
> which filled up the hollows, flooded the plain.

> "I'm leaving the many, I take but the twain
> of each dear species. Space but for two."
> So many behind, aboard so few!
> With only one Ark, what else could he do . . .

In my mother's version, however, the left-behind beasts were not without resources. Establishing a Committee for Staying Alive, they began to work to avoid drowning, each animal, "antler, snout, and bill," doing what it could:

> The beaver contributed splinter and chip.
> The woodpecker pounded so nothing would slip.
> The rhino cemented some cracks with his lip . . .

> Finally, their great labor completed,

> The animals crowded on top of the peak:
> worried and watery, weary and weak,
> too hungry to chatter, too hopeless to speak.

> They sighed. They shivered. They stood. They sat.
> They had raised up a mountain. Well, what of that?
> The cow said, "We're calling it A-RA-RAT."

Reader, I know you can guess what happened next.

SURFING and the consolations of philosophy. Consider lulls. Surfers very reluctant, always, to paddle in, sit waiting and waiting for one last wave. Stare at the horizon as if able to will a wave to appear, as if to turn for even a moment might undermine the entire effort. Still, one sees no deal being made, no propitiation of any god. Nonetheless, not a wave in sight, the "lull" going on and on. Which raises a question of semantics and, perhaps, metaphysics: how long can a lull persist and still be a lull?

Similarly, waves quite small, the surfer has cause to ponder one of Zeno's paradoxes, the notion that any moving object must reach the halfway point of a given course before it reaches the end. And that, because there are an infinite number of halfway points, the end can thus never be reached. Not in finite time, that is. Which is to say, from shore it may look like a lake out there at the lineup, but for the surfer sitting, waiting, hoping for something to ride, it may seem somewhat different. May seem, in fact, that the condition known as "flat" not only does not obtain at this particular moment, but that such a condition is, actually, a theoretical impossibility.

WATERBEDS, first surfacing in the late 1960s. Early models had problems: ruptures of the sac; too much weight for some floors; the water at room temperature too cold to sleep on. Nonetheless, acquiring heaters and baffles, for a while waterbeds were the rage, as much a part of the zeitgeist as . . . marijuana, with which they seemed somehow connected. Coterminous with first mass use of the word ecology, with the discovery of "Spaceship Earth," with Earth Shoes (which were to simulate standing in sand). Hot tubs soon to follow. And the waterbed's appeal? Comfort promised: adjusting to your contours, it would help bad backs, for example. And because of the rocking movement, there would be . . . better sex. More self-expression, yet another freedom.

By the mid-seventies, however, waterbeds had become something of an embarassment. Like platform shoes or bellbottoms. For the middle class, it was time to drain the waterbed for the last time, though some members of the working class were still buying theirs, a token of hipness and sexual freedom.

Now, in northern California, there are only a few entries for waterbeds in the Yellow Pages. A disappearing market, along with the special sheets, pads, and frames. It was just that brief moment in the history of our species—the use of pesticides at its zenith, ever more nuclear arms being tested and accumulated, the Vietnam War raging on television, the country still with money to burn—just that instant when there was this brand-new product for the consumer economy. Water to sleep on, and without even getting wet.

SAN FRANCISCO BAY, out once again on the long pier constructed in the twenties to accommodate ferries, this before completion of the Bay Bridge made it possible to drive east to west without circumnavigating south and around. The water is surprisingly shallow; they had to build out a great distance. Even the truncated section of pier still in use stretches more than half a mile, the rest of the original, abandoned and decrepit, running on beyond a gap cut to allow passage of small craft. Fishermen—Vietnamese, Cambodians, Latinos, blacks—crowd the railings casting and reeling in, crabs in buckets clambering over each other, sand sharks writhing on the pier's pavement, gulls perched on pilings, cormorants bobbing nearby, people cleaning their catch of small rays and leopard sharks on the concrete wash tables. Boats running before the southwest wind toward the nearby marina, many of them wing and wing—jib to one side, mainsail to the other, a flock of windsurfers on a broad reach just in front of them. Dead ahead, Angel Island, Alcatraz, and the Golden Gate Bridge, and, slightly off to the left, San Francisco, now several different shades of pale gray as night falls. Behind, to the east, the hills are already blue-black.

This enormous bay and its extraordinary rivers of fog, surrounded by five or seven (or now nine?) million human beings. Whose agents have for more than one hundred years been busily filling and polluting it. "The immense flocks of geese, ducks and pelicans, the great runs of salmon and steelhead, the enormous schools of smelt, the once numberless seals and whales are now a mere remnant," writes Malcolm Margolin. The herring fishing is almost gone, they say. And what of the century-old sturgeon in the Sacramento River, which runs down to the north end of the bay?

Once, at sunset out on the pier, a crazy man put a knife to my nephew's throat. The man was on drugs: angel dust, perhaps. So were his friends, one of whom approached us walking on his hands—walking on his hands? we were thinking—just before the assault, the light and water and disjointed violence like something out of Browning's film *Freaks*.

Such an attack while on the pier wasn't to be expected, but nor was it rare for this kind of man to be down there: for years the harbors sheltered wharf rats, people trying to get out of the larger human flow. A sprinkling of ex-cons from San Quentin (and its marvelous bay view!), released on the north side of the Richmond Bridge and making their way to some decrepit monohull that could provide cheap housing, the sense of a place where credit lines and phone lines just weren't important. Or people who'd quit their jobs to fix up a boat so they'd be able to sail around the world and be . . . free. (So recently the bay area was still the West, there was room to get lost in, roads not paved, San Francisco still a cowtown.) For some wharf rats, the outlaw feeling seemed reinforced not only by the way they made do but by their very proximity to nature, to the water, sun, fog. What, you see, what did some bureaucrat's laws have to do with all that?

Now, sometimes, watching yet another jet or helicopter come

over from Oakland or San Francisco or Alameda, taking in the car lights of evening gridlock on the noose of surrounding freeways and bridges, sometimes it seems that all that's been done to the bay was more than avarice, as if humankind had thought it over and concluded that the bay was just too wild to abide.

TOO MANY SURFERS at the surf line, relentlessly moving toward the rising swell, forestalling competitors. Predators, feeding on waves. Seen from below, surfers on their boards may appear—to sharks—like turtles. On whom they, the sharks, prey. Nonetheless, the pleasure of a friend's company out on the water: sharing both exhilaration and risk, sharing the reading of a given moment's options, imperatives. The hoot of triumph. The dolphin that leapt right in front of both of you as the wave formed.

And yet . . . "dawn patrol," paddling out by oneself at first light, most of the intense and layered lives of the city's highrises not quite conscious, morning papers not yet in the boxes, a few joggers circling Kapi'olani Park, sky rouged above Diamond Head, crescent moon up there riding its own waves. There can be at times the threat of too much solitude—what if one were always so alone in the face of such a wilderness?—but there is also the joy of responding to no other human ego, surfing with no look to the side to process the hungers—aggressions, affectations, dreams—of others, only swell becoming wave as it approaches the reef, sucking up, sucking up, higher, higher. Of course the correct—sane—response is to flee, but, since it is too late to run for shore, wave looming, the thing to do is paddle for your life *toward* it to get up and over. Then a momentary respite, with, sadly, the regrettable downside that you are now further out to sea. In such a quandary, instead of avoidance you might try this unnatural act: as the next vortex forms, move laterally, for position in what you divine will be the the cup of the approaching force, the sweet spot, they call it, *turn your back* just before the looming mass begins to break, paddle several times for momentum, and, leaping to your feet . . . take the drop, for a moment free or almost free of gravity, and then drive, *accelerate* down the face of the wave.

With—on solitary dawn patrol—no one there to see it, despite the tiers and tiers of windows on shore, no one at all.

No one, it turns out, except Bob, who's fixing up someone's water view apartment in lieu of rent. I bump into him at midday. "Hey, man, saw you out there this morning," Bob says, noncommittal as always.

Y OU KNOW THIS STORY TOO, how Moses was leading the people of Israel out of Egypt, and despite all that the Lord had visited upon the Egyptians—thunder and hail; a plague of locusts; a darkness over the land; the death of all first-born; etc. etc.—the stubborn Pharoah nonetheless overtook the people of Israel as they camped by the sea. But though the people of Israel feared for their lives, Moses followed the Lord's admonition, and "stretched out his hand over the sea; and the Lord drove the sea back by a strong east wind all night, and made the sea dry land, and the waters were divided. And the people of Israel went into the midst of the sea on dry ground, the waters being a wall to them on their right hand and on their left." Of course the Egyptian soldiers pursued them, but their chariots became bogged down, and then Moses, listening to the Lord, again stretched out his hand over the sea, and "The waters returned and covered the chariots and the horsemen and all the host of Pharoah that had followed them into the sea; not so much as one of them remained."

As Jesse Winchester sings, "Pharoah had an army, his horses shook the ground, / but mighty as that army was, to a man they drowned."

WATER AND MELANCHOLY. Robert Lowell's Atlantic high tide, which "Mutters to its hurt self, mutters and ebbs. / Waves wallow in their wash, go out and out, / Leave only the death-rattle of the crabs, / The beach increasing, its enormous snout / Sucking the ocean's side." Or Shakespeare's ruminations on ruin: "When I have seen the hungry ocean gain / Advantage on the kingdom of the shore, / And the firm soil win of the watery main, / Increasing store with loss and loss with store; / When I have seen such interchange of state, / Or state itself confounded to decay."

In Matthew Arnold's famous "Dover Beach," the poet, looking out at the English Channel, hears "the grating roar / Of pebbles the waves draw back, and fling / At their return, up the high strand, / Begin, and ease, and then again begin, / With tremulous cadence slow, and bring / The eternal note of sadness in." This, the poet asserts, was the very sound Sophocles heard long ago "and it brought / Into his mind the turbid ebb and flow / Of human misery." Which makes the poet think of "The sea of faith," which "Was once, too, at the full, and round earth's shore . . . But now I only hear / Its melancholy, long, withdrawing roar, / Retreating to the breath / Of the night-wind down the vast edges drear / And naked shingles of the world."

One wonders. Climate and mood. The English Channel is always cold. But could Sophocles really have had such bleak thoughts in, say, the Greek summer, before the autumn rains and *meltemi*, Poseidon earthshaker showing no malice, Aegean wine-dark at sunset, dolphins vaulting just offshore, the sea warmer, warmer with each passing day as the southern sun burned the chill from even a playwright's despairing bones?

Cetacean specialist Kenneth Norris writes that some 55 million years ago a "herd of mammals, somewhat reminiscent of small deer," chased fish in the water of an Asian estuary. These carnivores, free to enter areas until recently occupied by reptiles, would in time become "our whales and dolphins." And that Asian estuary? Well, it "led to a warm band of sea of enormous extent, girdling the globe, not far from the equator": the Tethys Sea (after the Titan Tethys, wife of Oceanus). One would guess it would have had to be very warm indeed, that estuary, to induce so miraculous a transition, so great a commitment.

As for a return to those halcyon days, however, we have Ballard's *The Drowned World*, set in the twenty-first century. Increased solar radiation has caused the polar caps to melt, humans retreating to the Arctic and Antarctic, the American Midwest now an enormous gulf, Europe a system of giant lagoons. There has also been "the growing ascendancy of amphibian and reptile forms best adapted to an aquatic life . . .,the genealogical tree of mankind was systematically pruning itself, apparently moving backwards in time, and a point might ultimately be reached where a second Adam and Eve found themselves alone in a new Eden."

As the outer landscape changes, organisms mutating for survival, Kerans, the novel's protagonist, experiences a sense of déjà vu. "Each one of us is as old as the entire biological kingdom," his friend Bodkin tells him, "and our bloodstreams are tributaries of the great sea of its total memory . . . the growing foetus recapitulates the entire evolutionary past, and its central nervous system is a coded time scale . . . the junction between the thoracic and lumbar vertebrae . . . is the great zone of transit between the gill-breathing fish and the air-breathing amphibians with their respiratory rib-cages . . . between the Paleozoic and Triassic Eras." Living in the tropical ruins of some drowned European capital, temperatures well over a hundred every day, Kerans is drawn back into mankind's remote biological past, its antediluvian—i.e., pre-Flood—consciousness.

And as for Robert Lowell's grim Atlantic, Shakespeare's ruminations, and the cold water musings of Matthew Arnold's "Dover Beach"? Well, not surprisingly, Ballard's vision of an ultratropical future brings Venice to mind, that city where mutability is already a good part of the appeal, entire cathedrals suddenly disappearing into water at any given angle. Particularly now that the latest scientific scare is global warming, a real threat to the atolls of so many island nations, one can surely be sobered even on a sunny summer day, even in the balm of waters with temperatures not too very far from our own 98.6.

T HE WATERS of my childhood, memories of which came to me on a tiny South Pacific island, perhaps eight by three miles, the villagers' houses right by the ocean, and though the nearest land—another small island—was some 250 miles away, here community was incredibly powerful, there really was no escaping one's neighbors, one's family. To go where? Which, strangely, sitting there on the mat in the canoe house watching the men play draughts, swatting flies with my fan, taking my turns with the kava *bilo*, set me thinking about Boston so many, many years before.

The water of my childhood. My friend George, tenant of his own aged aunt, who almost never emerged from her bedroom— George's parents had farmed out their children, and he ate alone every evening in a Beacon Street cafeteria frequented by the low-income single and elderly. George and I always walked to high school together, past old red-brick apartment buildings with tar driveways, sky inevitably gray, in muggy heat or in bitter cold, always the blind man selling papers, geometry hard, algebra easy, Latin relentless. In winter, George and I would sometimes skate after school on the nearby frozen reservoir, climbing the chain link fence, enormous nineteenth-century mansions on the hill above, blades chattering on the ridges of black ice as we were blown down toward Roxbury by the blustery winds.

The cold, then: In memory, the waters of my childhood always seem cold. (Forget the snow and sleet and hail and slush, water tending toward the solid, the closure it imposed, winter storms bringing the whole city to immobile silence; or our snowball fights; or the sledding; or the money my brother and I made shoveling out—exhuming!—neighbors' driveways and cars. Forget as well memories of collecting sea urchins in St. Croix in the Virgin Islands, the conch on our mantel at home for years after, or our mother leading us on a forced march around Bermuda for the sake of a possible poem.) In New England the lakes were cold until midsummer, and on the North shore of Boston—at Crane's Beach in particular—or Bar Harbor in Maine, or Nantucket, the water always incredibly cold. Children with no body fat at a great and shivering disadvantage, lips turning blue, bluer. Only the Cape, brushed by the Gulf Stream, was warmer, but our family seldom went there. Cold water, then (except in spring in high school with my girlfriend, hidden by the just-bloomed forsythia along the Muddy River, its waters surely affected by the fever of our mutual attraction). Cold water, and an odd correlative, that there seemed no body of water not class and ethnically defined. The Pilgrims had come to New England three hundred years earlier, and generations of immigrants since had divided it up, after the extirpation of the Indians, in fine and ever finer discriminations. For centuries in Boston they had been altering the water environment, the Charles River, for instance, long since controlled, rebuilt, reformed, polluted, the hills surrounding Boston Harbor long since levelled, the marshes filled, then occupied by mansions in Back Bay. And those big houses above the reservoir where George and I skated. Everywhere in New England there were big houses, and then houses less big, and everyone knew very, very well who had what. The nineteenth-century "cottages" with verandas and cupolas, the boat clubs and yachts and regattas, all of this spoke of access to water as a manifestation of social status, as if human hierarchies continued on and into the water, as if the great ocean itself was merely ancillary, something like, say, a polo field, simply one more arena in which to demonstrate privilege and power.

A<small>N</small> <small>AD</small> in *Honolulu Magazine,* for "the only swimming course designed for the truly phobic." Success guaranteed. Private classes, "goal oriented," with a "joint commitment to achieve your personal goals . . . Only from self mastery comes the confidence to relax and enjoy the water.")

They'd met, were in love. He'd always spent as much time as he could by the ocean, but, though a fine athlete, she didn't know how to swim. Or, she could swim, but was afraid to swim with her face in the water. Often she'd stay on shore when he went out.

One day he gave her a snorkel, showed her in shallow water how to use it, then added mask and flippers and wetsuit vest and went out with her to the reef, her hand on his shoulder as they pushed on. Now, breathing easily with the snorkel, suddenly she had no fear, was dazzled by the world beneath the surface, soon went out alone, though always he'd watch her carefully.

Some months later, spending the day at a hotel, having dozed for an hour in the sun, they stood by the wall at the shallow end of the pool, and she put her face in the water, head turning first left and then right as she did the upper portion of the Australian crawl. Without fear this time, since her feet were firmly planted.

Exhaling, hard, to allow each new sweet inhale. To her surprise, there was now no growing shortness of breath, no increasing panic, exhaustion. Within an hour she was doing lap after lap, her long, long arms taking stroke after stroke as if she could go on forever. She came out of the water grinning. "You looked like a swan," he told her.

Oh lovers: deep divers.

DROWNING AND MURDER. In Shakespeare's *Richard III*, the hunchback Duke of Gloucester, Richard, maneuvers Edward IV into imprisoning his own brother, the Duke of Clarence. Once in the tower, Clarence dreams that he is crossing the channel with his cousin Richard, but that

> . . . As we pac'd along
> Upon the giddy footing of the hatches,
> Methought that Gloucester stumbled; and, in falling,
> Struck me, that thought to stay him, overboard
> Into the tumbling billows of the main.
> O Lord! methought what pain it was to drown!
> What dreadful noise of water in mine ears!
> What ugly sights of death within mine eyes!

Shortly after this dream, Clarence is assassinated at Richard's instigation, one of the murderers saying as he stabs him that "if all this will not do/I'll drown you in the malmsey-butt." Later, near the end of the play, Richard is haunted by ghosts, including Clarence's, "I, that was wash'd to death with fulsome wine."

Water and suicide. Virginia Woolf, who left her walking stick on the bank of the River Ouse (pronounced *ooze*) near her country home, found a large stone, and put it into the pocket of her overcoat. Poet Hart Crane, overboard off a steamer 275 miles north of Havana. Overboard at two minutes before noon, wearing pajamas, from the main deck, other passengers watching. "[Crane] placed both hands on the railing, raised himself on his toes, and then dropped back again . . . Then, suddenly, he vaulted over the railing and jumped into the sea . . . Just once I saw Crane, swimming strongly, but never again." As Crane had written in his poem "Voyage-I", "The bottom of the sea is cruel."

There is also Edna at the end of Chopin's *The Awakening*, naked with the Gulf stretched out before her "gleaming with the million lights of the sun," the voice of the sea "seductive, never ceasing, whispering, clamoring, murmuring." And Jack London's Martin Eden, who worked at it. Having slipped out of a porthole and into the ocean, Eden watched the lights of the steamer growing dim, but noticed that he was swimming "as though it were his intention to make for the nearest land a thousand miles or so away." Diving down, he inhaled some water, but "quite involuntarily his arms and legs clawed . . . and drove him up to the surface." Finally, filling his lungs with air, "Down, down he swam till his arms and legs grew tired and hardly moved . . . but he compelled [them] to drive him deeper until his will snapped and the air drove from his lungs in a great explosive rush . . . Then came pain and strangulation . . . His wilful hands and feet began to beat and churn about, spasmodically and feebly. But he had fooled them and the will to live that made them beat and churn. He was too deep down. They could never bring him to the surface."

And then there's Ophelia. In *Hamlet*, you remember, the prince has accidentally killed Polonius; Ophelia, Polonius's daughter, who loves Hamlet, has gone crazy; and Laertes,

Polonius's son, vows vengeance. At this moment the queen, Hamlet's mother, comes in to tell Laertes and her husband the king that Ophelia has drowned.

> . . . an envious sliver broke,
> When down her weedy trophies and herself
> Fell in the weeping brook. Her clothes spread wide;
> And, mermaid-like, awhile they bore her up:
> Which time she chanted snatches of old tunes,
> As one incapable of her own distress,
> Or like a creature native and indu'd
> Unto that element: but long it could not be
> Till that her garments, heavy with their drink,
> Pull'd the poor wretch from her melodious lay
> To muddy death.

It turns out, however, that the Queen's version of Ophelia's death is not true. How can she be given a Christian burial, one of the gravediggers asks, "unless she drowned herself in her own defence?"

> 1 CLOWN It must be *se offendendo;* it cannot be else. For here lies the point: if I drown myself wittingly, it argues an act: and an act hath three branches; it is to act, to do, and to perform: argal, she drowned herself wittingly.
> 2 CLOWN Nay, but hear you, goodman delver—,
> 1 CLOWN Give me leave. Here lies the water; good: here stands the man; good: if the man go to this water and drown himself, it is, will he nill he, he goes—mark you that: but if the water come to him and drown him, he drowns not himself.

Water and suicide. There are also the nearly one thousand people who have jumped from the Golden Gate Bridge since it opened in 1937. In 1938, a refugee from Germany, apparently despairing of the fate of relatives she'd left behind, climbed over the railing. In 1945, a father told his five-year-old daughter to jump. Then he followed her. As for latter-day jumpers, one reads about them in the morning *Chronicle.* "Man Chose Death Over 'Serving Reagan' " was one headline. This jumper met his wife at a Star Trek convention in Los Angeles. His wife said her husband had a fantasy of sitting on the bridge and lecturing people about the world's problems.

From the nearly posthumous remarks of the more than fifteen jumpers known to have survived, they envisioned such a sea death as clean, gentle, not at all violent. It should be added that they all jumped facing east—toward land—rather than west, perhaps the better to address the human community with their final act, or perhaps simply because to face the open ocean was too clear a vision of the vastness to come.

Water and murder, water and suicide. Magnate Robert Maxwell's mysterious yachting death, it seems, might have been neither murder nor suicide, but rather a case of calenture: the impulse, long known to mariners, to jump into the sea. Not caused by sunstroke, not an infection, not a personal psychological malady, though calenture is often defined as due to excessive heat, a fever with delirium. One other definition, however, puts calenture well in the past, saying it was a fever "formerly supposed to affect sailors in the tropics, causing them to imagine the sea a green field and to leap into it."

Scanning the cable TV dial, one often encounters half-hour-long paid presentations by Dave Del Dotto (hosted by John Davidson—how the mighty have fallen!), an entrepreneur who offers a way to get rich buying real estate. Knowing how to sell success, Del Dotto has his pitches filmed on Waikiki, *lei* around his neck, Pacific at his back.

Such use of the ocean makes one think of Wyland: a familiar one-word name in Hawai'i, a fellow who bills himself as America's leading environmental artist. "If people see the beauty in nature," Wyland says, "I feel they will work to preserve it before it's too late." Wyland, who conveys something of a Tom Selleck look (Selleck, the mustachioed protagonist of *Magnum P.I.*, a TV series set in Hawai'i), has painted "nineteen life-size whale walls throughout the United States, Canada, Australia, Japan, and Europe," and aspires to another eighty-one. (Though there is no whaling in Wyland's murals, and though there is no connection to Jerusalem, the murals are often referred to as Whaling Walls.)

You've seen Wyland's art, many of his works cross-sections above and below the surface, no fish eating any other, often a sunset in progress, colors edging toward the garish, everything as unsentimental as a sixties Keene print, those wide honest eyes staring right at your aorta. Art, they say, should imply risk, be a process of learning for the artist, but though Wyland apparently spends time underwater "researching" what his paintings will "reflect," it's hard to avoid thinking he has not intended to bleed the mystery out of his subject, hard to imagine he's discovering such bathos in the benthos. But who knows? Believing is seeing.

A somewhat different kind of whale artist is Larry Foster, who as a child was taken by his parents down to the Sacramento train station to look at a whale displayed on a flatcar. "I could see it was large and black, but I never did see the whale. Where is the mammal? . . . It was a fin whale and it was on its side. We reached the mouth, which was open and cavernous. On the right side there were many pleats, or wrinkles, like the world's worst accordion band accident, and on the left side there was giant fur or something. That was the baleen. But at the time I left disappointed."

By the early 1960s, Foster writes, "whale curiosity got the best of me. I quit my job . . . got a divorce, and moved into a warehouse with no windows . . . The object was to find out what the largest animals in the world look like." Studying photographs, Foster discovered that representations of whales were simply not true even to the known anatomical facts. As he explains, the problem of depicting whales is that one "cannot study or, in most cases, even *see* the subject." Whale photographs, though now far more common, still tend to be mostly of several accessible species. Dead whales on land, of course, are not only not alive but subject to forces they are free of in water. Finally, whale skeletons do not suggest the whales' external shapes.

Foster has spent most of the last twenty-five years drawing

and painting cetaceans. Only cetaceans. He is, however, seldom if ever in the water, working instead from photographs and anatomical descriptions. "Studying live whales at sea is fraught with difficulty," he argues, and of course in the water one can catch only glimpses of portions of so large a creature. Nonetheless, Foster's obsession with accurately representing cetaceans seems paralleled by a need to keep his distance, as if only staying *out* of the water enables his vision of these creatures who live in it. As if being in the water with whales would not only not be helpful but somehow inimical to his extraordinary effort to portray them.

Recently, Foster did a chart in which, asked to include the land mammals that became whales, he had to depict a bison. As he explains, this was "the first time in my life I have ever had to paint fur." Though Foster has been called the Audubon of whales, he sidesteps the compliment, responding, "I say I'm more like the Birdman of Alcatraz."

Y EARS AGO, when I was first traveling in the Pacific, Hawai'i seemed to me the westernmost point of the United States. A colony, yes, but American. Avis, MacDonald's, Hertz, Hilton, United. A further California. But then one day, jogging in Kapi'olani Park in Honolulu, in the shadow of Diamond Head, I stopped to watch an incredibly violent rugby game, one team Samoans, the other Tongans. And, suddenly, it came clear: Hawai'i was the northeastern corner of Polynesia, Easter Island the southeastern corner, the Marquesas, Tahiti, Tonga, Samoa, and New Zealand thus Polynesian points west and south. Honolulu, in this view, a kind of Rome of the Pacific, various islanders making their way north and east to the imperial city.

Imagine the exploration and colonization of the Pacific—"a third of the Earth," as Kenneth Brower calls it—by Polynesians and Melanesians, "out on the monotonous blue, when the horizon had come back around to meet itself and obliterate land behind them." Their "canoes" often seventy to one hundred feet long, "longer and faster than the . . . European vessels that first came among them." When Captain Cook arrived at Kealakekua Bay, for instance, he was surrounded by three thousand "canoes." In a particularly bravura section of his *A Song for*

Satawal, Brower chants the evolution over millennia—and dispersion through Oceania—of this vehicle "for all the human speciation," which was itself "speciating all the while . . . Of the thousands of dead ends and wrong turns . . . impasses and retrogressions, we have no record." Of the terminal stages of dispersion, however, witnessed by whites, we do know something. The canoe paddle, for instance, "had become ovate in Fiji, approximately ovate in Hawaii, an elongated oval at the Torres Straits, and an elongated oval painted with red-and-black human faces in the northwestern Solomons. It was a fine-pointed oval painted like a fish in the southeastern Solomons and a broad oval with a beaklike tip in the Marquesas. It was obovate in Raivavai, spatulate in Tuamotu, lanceolate in Nauru, broadly lanceolate in Rapa, lanceolate with acuminate tips in the Carolines, lanceolate and plano-convex in cross section in New Zealand, lanceolate and stiletto thin in the Tanga group of the Bismarck Archipelago, lanceolate and lightly carved in the Mailu Islands, lanceolate and decorated with carved snakes in New Ireland, lanceolate and inlaid with disks of pearl shell in Manihiki. It was diamond-shaped at Cape Direction of Queensland, heart-shaped in Orokaiva, spade-shaped in the Hermit Islands, banana-leaf-shaped in Mangareva, and fountain-pen-nib-shaped in the Cook Islands."

On Easter Island, Brower concludes, "that remotest and easternmost of Polynesia's outposts," timber for building canoes was used up, and the paddles "suffered a devolution, or perhaps it was a sublimation. The Easter Island paddle was double-bladed, like a kayak paddle, but with hardly any shaft separating the blades. One blade of each pair was decorated, and the other was plain. The decorated blade was carved in low relief into a radically simplified semblance of a human face, and in some paddles the face was painted with black-and-white patterns identical to the facial tattoos of the Marquesas, the ancestral homeland. The plain blade of each pair was obovate and businesslike. With a longer shaft, and without the encumbrance of its tattooed twin, it might actually have propelled a canoe."

The Polynesian past. History is, as they say, written by the victors, but it is also a Rorschach test: we read in it what we are able to see. By 1870, after a century of contact with Europeans, there were perhaps forty thousand native Hawaiians, down from a population that may have been more than five hundred thousand. There was now also leprosy, which Hawaiians called *ma'i-Pākē*, Chinese disease. Transmitted by the imported Chinese laborers or not, leprosy as the Hawaiians well knew came from outside. Despite the developing science of bacteriology, no vaccine had been devised for the recently discovered *bacillus leprae*. Many *haoles*, Gavin Daws explains, believed leprosy was associated with venereal disease or a form of it: Hawaiians were promiscuous, their leprosy thus "as much a judgment as a disease." (Of course, Captain Cook's expedition, which had brought syphilis to Hawai'i, knew it.) Though only one hundred whites contracted leprosy in Hawai'i in the nineteenth century, it seemed to some merchants to threaten the "total destruction of civilization, property values, and industry." At the personal level, this could mean terror. Sanford Ballard Dole's wife, Ana, "led a private life dominated by such a dread of leprosy that she would not go from room to room in her own house without covering the doorknob with a handkerchief." (Though an infectious disease, leprosy is in fact one of the least communicable.)

In 1865 the Hawai'i legislature began transporting the afflicted to the Kalawao settlement on Moloka'i. Within fifteen years more than a thousand had been sent; in all, more than eight thousand. Many refused to work; there was robbery of the sick and dying. Thus, the cry emanating from Kalawao was " 'A 'ole kanawai ma keia wahi"—"In this place there is no law." Though many whites believed that without segregation Hawai'i would become a "nation of lepers," native Hawaiians were not repelled by the afflicted, seemed in fact to consider segregation worse than the disease. Further, Daws writes, "hundreds of healthy Hawaiians, faced with the exile of a friend or relative . . . chose to go too, to help, to kokua . . . in the early days, there were as many kokua as there were people with the disease." This, though, in the 1870s "never less often than two or three times a week, someone died." (Daws also writes that in the early history of the settlement there was only a single white kōkua—other than Father Damien, the Catholic priest.) (Not only were there very few suicides at Kalawao, but apparently some Hawaiians even sought to simulate the marks of the disease.)

Against this backdrop, there is the famous story of Ko'olau the leper. In 1893, at Kalalau Valley on the island of Kaua'i, the cowboy Ko'olau shot and killed the haole sheriff, Stolz, who sought to transport him to Moloka'i without his wife and child. Ko'olau then also shot and killed two of a party of eighty soldiers who came after him, and soon after disappeared with his wife and child. In 1906 his wife, Pi'ilani, published in Hawaiian an account of the death of her husband and child. As it turns out, they never left the Kalalau Valley, but remained in hiding in what Pi'ilani called (in Frazier's translation) "the gloom of the mountain forest," where "we were as wild things." After nearly two years their son died of leprosy: "How can I tell of the grief that overcame the parents, alone in the wilderness?" Pi'ilani writes. Worse, she could see her husband begin to fail. A year later, "in the middle of the night, during the turning of the Milky Way, the light in the house that was Kalua-i-Koolau was extinguished . . . leaving only his clay behind for me to lament over—I alone in the awesome loneliness which was peopled only with the voices of the land shells, which seemed to lament with me in those hours before the break of dawn." *Auwē, auwē.*

J ACK THE SURFER. Surfing for him something about hunting the waves, or, occasionally, being hunted by them. Turning forty, still living right across from the beach in Carlsbad, in the water on dawn patrol nearly every morning. Not a beach bum, however: he has a job selling fine mountain gear, a good job as jobs go—flexible workdays, ample vacation time. Work chosen to allow him to continue to surf. Work long since pleasant, boring, unfulfilling.

When his wife accuses him yet again of being a Peter Pan, he finally goes to see his wife's psychologist, a woman. A compulsive triathlete, the therapist concludes that Jack's responsible enough, says his wife is lucky to have someone so physically fit with a passion for nature. Pleased, relieved, Jack nonetheless wonders. At a meeting of the sales force at his company, one of the managers notices that Jack's monthly calendar is also a tide chart, and teases him. Jack can read the component of envy, of course, but still . . . is surfing enough to define—to defend— a life?

Jack at forty, remembering surfing as a way to leave behind an overworked mother and an absent father. Being out on the water, thinking only of the waves. Remembering Tavarua, in

Fiji, bunking with surf nazis from the States and Australia, riding almost perfect sets day after day. Being the only one there reading a book. Reading anything. And, now, turning forty, wondering why it should be more strange to know the time of the next high tide than to know, say, that the network news will be on at seven.

O F THE OCEAN, "the mother of life on this earth as surely as the sun is the father," Joana Vawara writes, "I believe her to be the essential doctor, the great healer, cleansing body and mind, restoring soul and circulation . . . The warm salt water washes away dirt and infection . . . relieves tired joints and bones from the continuous necessity of holding up our weight, gives us the freedom to fly."

Taking the waters. For Dian Buchman, Ph.D., the day begins with two glasses of *cold* water about an hour before breakfast, and marching "for a few minutes in a shallow *cold* foot bath." Water can be used therapeutically, she writes, for everything from Acne and Achilles Tendon injuries to Colitis ("Apply a hot moist compress to abdomen" for spasm; for gas, "Apply a cold wet pack to abdomen, cover with dry towel, and cover the entire body with warm bedclothes") to Varicose Veins (hot sage tea compresses). For Writer's Cramp Dr. Buchanan recommends "a percussion shower spray of alternate long hot and then short cold water to the hand."

J. V. Cerney, A.B., D.M., D.P.M., a podiatrist whose books include *How to Develop a Million Dollar Personality* and *Talk Your Way to Success,* is also the author of *Modern Magic of Natural Healing with*

Water Therapy, in which he offers the secrets of famous European doctors. For example, a cold "fan douche"—spray from a nozzle attached to a hose—applied to the lower back and tailbone revitalizes "sex life." And the "amazing Neptune's Girdle," Cerny writes, is the water cure for dilated stomach. (Soak a sheet in cold water, wring it out, and wrap it around the waist. Go to sleep. Change the dressing as it becomes warm.)

Such prescriptions have a long lineage in the United States, going back at least to the nineteenth-century hydropathic movement, which, as Catherine Albanese explains, "saw 'pure' water as the primary healing agent for illness of whatever sort." This was a gospel, requiring spreading of the Good News: "Wash, and be healed." According to one hydropath, apostles would give people "God's regenerating truth . . . And they will apply Water-Cure . . . to heal their patients of the diseases consequent upon hereditary taint, or in other words 'original sin' and the actual transgression in their own lives." According to another hydropath, the millennium was at hand: "Like the silent dewy shower which is now falling on the physical world, water will descend on the moral world, dispersing its fogs of gloom, refreshing the landscape of society, revealing the sun of temperance, and reviving the withering flowers of humanity." (All this must be weighed against conventional medicine, which then practiced blood-letting, and held that women were hampered by menstrual problems and intellectually inferior to men. Hydropathy, by contrast, saw women's physiology as normal, opposed drastic remedies, and prescribed rest, changes in diet, temperance, and exercise. As Susan Cayleff explains, hydropathy also encouraged "a deemphasis of the physician-patient relationship" while soliciting female physicians, and "became a retreat for the nineteenth-century woman searching for an alternative philoso-

phy that stressed her capabilities, strengths, and potentialities."
Often the retreats were marked by a supportive ambience for
women, and/or simply a respite from the rigors of domestic life
and frequent pregnancies.)

Though not myself a millennarian, as the son of a doctor I
have over the years devised and practiced various forms of water
therapy, including swimming therapy, surfing therapy, kayaking
therapy, sailing therapy, and snorkeling therapy. Usually, however, if only as a form of verbal economy, I prescribe holding
the word *therapy* in the sense that one might "hold the mayo" on
a tuna sub. As for other healing waters I've been in, I cherish the
memory of some wonderful evenings in the mid-sixties in the
tubs at Esalen on Big Sur. Late at night, after the paying
customers had finished their day of building being, denizens of
the neighboring canyons and crevices would slip down to the
bath house, which hung on a cliff over the Pacific. There, they'd
undress: nudity was *de rigeur.* Checking each other out, they'd
clamber into the tubs, pondering the ineffable relationship between bathing and Eros, immersing themselves in water that was
clearly—yes!—therapeutic.

Years later, I had reason to regret ever having left the baths,
and not just because I so enjoyed the sight of the nude female
form that seemed an inescapable corollary of the healing waters.
No, sad to say, there are two countries, health and illness, and
in some unheroic, even foolish, way I had passed from the
former to the latter. A sequence of endless flus, staph infections,
and rounds of antibiotics, capped off with penumonia that left
me weak as a baby. Months lost in this banal but too real
syndrome. I could not escape the feeling I'd been doing some
sort of violence to myself, that I was no longer able to live the
life I'd long assumed I could handle. Poisons of the modern

urban environment? Or simply my capacity to handle that environment? It was to the water—to the warm ocean—that I returned to heal.

And what had kept me away so long, you might ask? Oh, well, I'd been busy, had built a life, was pursuing my vocation as a writer. My plate was full. But beyond that, there had always been a point at which the ocean not only brought me great joy but threatened to wash me away. A point, too, when one's stay in the tropics seemed too long, when one began to envision the melodramatic possibility of a Conradian or Maughamian fate. But now, sick and exhausted with being sick, I had no great fear of the risk of dissolution, little concern that I'd end up an outcast of the islands. I descended the sea ladder each day, lay down in the water, rising and falling in the swell. Yes, water therapy.

IN THE DEEP BLUE off Diamond Head, running downwind before the howling trades, kayak all too eager to pitchpole, to broach. The waves, also wind-inspired, giving chase. *A following sea.*

"The shark was perhaps the most universally worshipped
of all the 'aumakuas ... Each of the sharks, too, had its
kahu (keeper), who was responsible for its care and worship ... The shark enjoyed the caresses of its *kahu* as it
came ... to receive a pig, a fowl ... or some other
substantial token of its *kahu*'s devotion. And in turn it
was always ready to assist the *kahu*, guarding him from
any danger ..."

—J. S. EMERSON

A WOMAN SWIMMING in front of her home at Olowalu
on Maui is killed by a fifteen-foot tiger shark. When the State
starts to underwrite a hunt, some native Hawaiians protest that
sharks can be family gods, though apparently few Hawaiians are
now able to identify their particular shark or even species of
shark. In the course of debate, it is pointed out that of course
Hawaiians traditionally fished for sharks, made drums, knives,
and hooks from their carcasses, and that there are more than
twenty kinds of sharks in Hawai'i. (Hawaiian fishermen were

skilled enough to rope sharks they'd fed and drugged, even to ride them like horses, but sharks could also take human form, become *manō kānaka,* shark men.) Were tiger sharks, for instance, ever *'aumakua*? Finally, a large shark is caught where the woman was killed, but there is no evidence—that is, no body parts in its stomach, no clothing—that this was the shark in question.

Also, during the course of public response to the attack, it is argued that there have been at most 85 documented attacks in Hawai'i over the last 200 years, with 36 fatalities, only 1.5 attacks/year over the past 40 years (and even these statistics, some feel, overstate the menace by recording attacks after drownings). Marine biologist Rick Martini, quoted in the *Honolulu Weekly,* said, apropos of suicide statistics in Hawai'i: "you are two hundred times more likely to kill yourself than to get attacked by a shark."

When sighting a shark, according to icthyologist Arnold Suzumoto, one should remain calm and "swim like a human," since people are "not really on the diet of sharks." (It is also "probably true," Suzumoto writes, "that people have more intense fears of sharks than sharks do of people." Perhaps. Seen by a fish, Joseph Brodsky argues, man will appear if not an octopus than a quadropus. "Should one ask a simple *orata* . . . what it thinks one looks like, it will reply, You are a monster.")

In the days after the woman's death, many people talk of the attack. She—her name was Martha Morell—went swimming in murky water, they suggest, a great mistake; or, Olowalu is well-known for its shark population. The brunt of much of this discussion is that the woman, an immigrant from the mainland, was somehow responsible, should have known better. "I guess she thought she had the power," a local surfer tells me as we sit out at the break. Later, on the seawall, a woman says, "It was written," meaning that this was part of the victim's karma, a form of compensation for actions in a previous life. Hearing these responses to the death of Martha Morell, it becomes hard not to feel that the real fear for most people is that the shark attack was just random. Their ongoing psychological effort thus to ward off the possibility that, to recast a recent idiom, "Sharks happen."

(Months later, testament to the intricate racial politics of Hawai'i, a rumor circulates that the victim had forbidden some locals access across her land to the beach. According to this rumor, these locals then dumped the carcass of a cow in the water in order to attract predators. Though this rumor seems essentially an expression of intraspecies anxiety or malice on terra firma, having little to do with the ocean or its creatures, it is true that public support for shark eradication—and sympathy for the victim—increases when a local boogie-boarder, a teenage boy, is fatally attacked by a tiger shark in the shore break at midday, that is, at a time and place when, according to conventional wisdom, it was unlikely to occur.)

How holy people look," wrote Samuel Butler, "when they are seasick! There was a patient Parsee near me who seemed purified once and for ever from all taint of the flesh. Buddha was a low, worldly minded, music-hall comic singer in comparison. He sat like this for a long time . . . [until] he made a noise like cows coming home to be milked on an April evening."

I myself have been seasick not only on a sailing vessel off the coast of California but off the northern coast of Ireland, en route to Tory Island in the dead of winter, launch packed to the gills with local folk, skipper's boozy breath mixing with the vapor of gasoline to send me to the gunwhale. And years before that, crossing the English Channel, ferry pitching and rolling, waves green and black and very large, two hundred Boy Scouts in uniform on deck heading home from Calais to Dover, all of us having consumed too many *gâteaux*, the 201 of us in unison then rushed to the rail to give back to the inexorable sea that divine custard, cream, and chocolate. "Seasickness," the merciless Butler also wrote, ". . . is the inarticulate expression of the pain we feel of seeing a proselyte escape us just as we were on the point of converting it." (In Rupert Brooke's poem "Channel

Passage," the narrator's options, as he tries to focus on something *not* on the boat, come down to a choice "twixt love and nausea," to a "sea-sick body, or a you-sick soul.") Quite judiciously, Charles Darwin pointed out that "If a person suffer much from seasickness, let him weigh it heavily in the balance. I speak from experience: it is no trifling evil, cured in a week." (Darwin perhaps spent too much time at sea. "And what are the boasted glories of the illimitable ocean?" he wrote. "A tedious waste, a desert of water, as the Arabian calls it.")

Seasickness, not quite the same as getting overwhelmed by and so avoiding, or becoming queasy about—even sick of—the ocean. "When does a man quit the sea?" asks E. B. White, speaking of the point at which the aging sailor has "lost touch with the wind." After too much time surfing, for instance, arms exhausted, belly rash from the wax, abraded nipples, infected coral cuts on hands and feet, nose dripping, after all this there's the great relief of a day not out at the break. Or think of people in Hawai'i who go to the ocean so seldom—though they do swim in pools, water well chlorinated—that one senses *something* is being avoided. Does the very sight of the ocean undercut the rhythms and premises of a twentieth-century terrestrial life? Denying the kinds of control essential to consumer society? Or consider Joseph Conrad, who spent more than twenty years in the merchant marine and then wrote stories deriving from that life. Apparently Conrad chose to be landlocked when he came ashore in England, a ship's captain become writer, Pole writing in English. Ford Maddox Ford said his friend Conrad "detested the sea as a man detests a cast-off mistress . . . his passion became to live out of sight of the sea and all its memories." (Is Ford correct? Did Conrad not often sail with friends on their yachts after leaving the merchant marine?) If so, Conrad would seem hardly original: he was much like the proverbial sailor who, days at sea finally over, carries a small anchor on his back as he heads inland looking for a place to light, walking and waiting until finally someone asks, "What's that?"

Though the ocean, as Watson writes, "is part of a water network, a continuous liquid web that holds our lives together," though "the long ancestral lines of every plant and animal in the world began in the ocean," though "the sea is our mother, her cadence . . . part of our unconscious . . . there is a very real sense in which salt water is inhuman. It fails in the first duty of water, which is . . . to nourish us." By which he refers to the fact that a "drop of 2 percent in our body fluid immediately manifests itself as thirst or pain; a 5 percent loss induces hallucinations; and a loss of just 12 percent is lethal." But beyond this, there is simply a point at which it is all too much, where one has had enough. As Tony Quagliano writes, "Sooner or later you have to get off the beach." Or there is the dazed state of the surfer who has been out in the waves too long, the question periodically coming to mind as he sits there between sets asking himself, "What's the goal here? In? Out?" Paddling *in*, finally: an act of unexpected clarity. The great relief, the next morning, of an absolutely flat day, respite at long last from Valery's *"La mer, la mer, toujours recommencée!"*

After weeks of only a bathing suit or perhaps also a tanktop, bare feet or rubber "slippers," the freedom of life in or near water having begun to feel not just simpler or more pure but like regression—a not entirely pleasant sensation—after all this, finally into dungarees *mit* belt with silver fittings; moray eel T-shirt (orange on black); *very* comfortable Nike Air running shoes; denim jacket. Amazed to experience the amplification clothes bestow, the opulent extension of the self, to realize how much the water had almost washed away.

Thus dressed, there is still the need for something more after

too much battering from—having been given a drenching by—
the waves. (Drenched: to wet thoroughly, to steep, to soak. As
a child in Boston, coming in from the inevitable rain, I'd stand
in the back porch room dripping, my mother surveying the
damage: "You're drenched," she'd say. Some years later, working
on a ranch, I "drenched"—forcibly administered medicine to—
sheep and cattle.) These days, after too many waves, I am
consoled by sushi, sashimi, sake, and green tea. The conjunction
of pelagic food only recently alive with the decorum and intricate artifice of its presentation, the insistence on appreciation of
the food's color, shape, texture. If cooking is adding heat to
food, to keep it raw is to insist on its distance from the
domestic. Yet in sushi the natural is laboriously *prepared*, hands-
on, fish carefully sliced, rice shaped and molded—seventeen
steps in forming one order of *nigiri-zushi*, they say—even what
is most wild arranged, made beautiful, celebrated in human
terms. Consider *fugu*, blowfish: a much-prized delicacy, white
flesh that is almost transparent when sliced thin, nearly disappearing on the plate, sweet but bestowing a slight numbness on
lips and tongue when consumed, a beautiful, evasive fish that can
kill if you eat, say, its liver or ovaries at the wrong time of year.
(The first sign of poisoning? The diner dropping his chopsticks
as the tetrodotoxin begins its attack on the central nervous
system.)

The sushi bar's immaculate cypress counter. The sake cups.
The *wasabi*. One round, another, another, of the small portions,
each suggesting yet more to come, suggesting time to be given
over to this place, occasion. The Shinto resonances too: spare
wood counter evoking the shrines; sake and the rice as links to
the deities of nature. "Water," says the Taoist sushi chef, thinking it over, "nothing can contain it." And, "If water has a desire,
its desire is to come down." And, "The ocean depths, who's to

find the bottom?" And, he says, "Water is an evocation, on the manifest side, of the elusive Nothingness."

Here in the States, of course, many people don't much like to eat fish, are quick to tell you so, even quicker to say they don't know how *anyone* can eat raw fish. My dentist's assistant, pregnant with a very fishy fetus, makes a face at the very mention of the word "sushi." (I do not, then, speak of goldfish-swallowing contests when I was young, much less of the traditional Polynesian practice of eating live fish.) But why argue about taste? One man's fish . . .

Nonetheless, after too much time in the waves, in too deep, in over my head, finally on dry land, clothed once more . . . thus evolved, I fight fire with fire: more *uni;* that succulent *hamachi;* some *tobiko;* and, please . . . one more order of *mirugai.*

WAIKĪKĪ: Tourists from Japan, Europe, and the mainland, many stopping to pose for photographs in front of the statue of Duke Kahanamoku (1890–1968), taking on a bit of his *mana*. Olympic champion in swimming, great surfer, actor in many Hollywood films, Kahanamoku was the paradigm of the Hawaiian waterman.

As described in Timmons's *Waikiki Beachboy*, Kahanamoku grew up across from the beach. As his brother Louis said, "My family believes we come from the ocean. And that's where we're going back." Or, according to Kenneth Brown, "He was no more afraid of what might happen to him at sea than you or I would be of getting hit by a car crossing the street." Yet he was also, Timmons writes, "as unfathomable out of the water as he was fearless in it . . . He had a mind that saw deeply and in detail, but he was very contained, reticent to a fault. Like the vast ocean itself, he seemed for the most part to exist below the surface." As Kenneth Brown argues, " 'Duke was completely transparent. No phoniness . . . People could say to you that Duke was simple—the bugga must be dumb! No way . . . Duke was totally without guile. He knew a lot of things.' " Perhaps it was simply that out of the water, as George McPherson put it, Duke was out of his element.

A local boy who made good, world famous by the time he was in his early twenties, dominating swimming the way Jim Thorpe then dominated track and field, Kanahamoku seemed trapped by fame, could never again simply live the life of a waterman. When he died, his ashes were strewn off Waikīkī. As one of his brothers later said, "Duke was never afraid of the blue water."

Not long after his return to California from time in the tropics, wondering again if he should not move to warm water once and for all, he put a bag of scuba gear in the car to loan to a friend heading for Hawai'i. Snorkels, masks, wet suits, flippers. None of it new, but all in good shape. He thought about moving the equipment to the trunk as he went off to do an errand, but it was midday on a busy street. When he came back, his car had been broken into; the bag was gone, as well as his jacket and some tools. Berating himself, he called the police, itemizing what had been stolen. He then called his insurance company, told them he estimated the value of the gear at nine hundred and fifty dollars, learned he had a thousand-dollar deductible. A friend suggested going down to the local flea market. The thief would turn the gear over immediately, the friend explained; it would turn up there. For sale, cheap.

Some weeks later, the bag surfaced in the Lost and Found of a church across the street from where the break-in had occurred. The thief had apparently examined the contents of the bag and jettisoned it. Nothing was lost, nothing.

He was glad not to have to pay to replace the equipment. Still, dreaming of the waves each night, happy to see his friends but feeling too far from the warm ocean, this thought kept intruding, that it was strange to be spending time in a place where water gear could appear to have neither function nor value.

F ORGET FOR A MOMENT the raging male sea, read by John Fowles as both *superego* and *id*, at once beyond all control and "punisher of presumption." Consider the sea in its female aspect. Some male shredders, perennial adolescents, say surfing is like sex. (See Mr. Zogs Sex Wax—wax making the board's surface less slippery—"The Best for Your Stick.") Not that surfers get sex as a result of surfing, all those admiring women back on the beach, but that surfing is like sex. Waves of orgasm? Entering the tube? "It's like sex without guilt," one man puts it, "like safe sex." "Get a grip," another surfer responds; "surfing is like surfing." Perhaps, then, the notion of a relationship between surfing and sex works better in reverse. As the late, great Rap Reiplinger intoned on his album *Poi Dog*, "Loving you is surfing you."

Males and the water: The sea as maternal; the sea as one's mistress; the lure of mermaids, those ambiguous creatures; traditional prohibitions on Polynesian men against having sex before leaving shore to fish; sirens singing, Odysseus strapped to the mast (was their melody—perhaps the song of whales in the Mediterranean—intended to drive one mad, or, as Kafka suggested, the sound of true knowledge?). In all this do we have no more than male fear of the Other, of women as Nature, or is there something specific to water? Water, which, Joseph Brodsky argues, "reflects and refracts everything, including itself, alternating forms and substances, sometimes gently, sometimes monstrously."

For Brodsky, creatures like mermaids "are our self-portraits, in the sense that they denote the species' genetic memory of evolution." A notion that evokes the work of psychoanalyst Sandor Ferenczi. "I will refer to the peculiar fact," wrote Ferenczi, "that the genital secretion of the female among the high mammals . . . possesses a distinctly fishy odor." In offering this, Ferenczi was not about to tell us something about, say, summer nights during his adolescence in Hungary. Analyzed by and then colleague of Sigmund Freud, Ferenczi (1873–1933) was an early diver in the ocean of psychoanalytic theory. In *Thalassa: A Theory of Genitality*, he postulated that the wish to return to the womb and its amniotic fluids symbolizes a wish to return to the sea itself. "What," he asked, "if the entire intrauterine existence of the higher mammals were only a replica of the type of existence [of] that aboriginal piscine period, and birth itself, nothing but a recapitulation on the part of the individual of the great catastrophe which at the time of the recession of the ocean forced so many animals . . . to adapt themselves to a land existence." Against his own psyche's "resistances," Ferenzci bravely argued that:

- sleep and sex are regressions to the womb and "that proto-type of everything maternal, the sea";
- since the [male] individual identifies with both the penis in the vagina and sperm "swarming into the body of the female, he also repeats symbolically the danger of death" his animal ancestors overcame in the cataclysmic drying up of the sea;

- penises first developed in amphibians and reptiles "as a result of the striving to restore the lost mode of life in a moist milieu";
- placental gill-breathing in human embryos demonstrates that "the striving in the direction of an aquatic mode of life is never completely given up."

Speaking of reading dreams of rescue from water as representations of birth and coitus, Ferenczi concluded that at the phylogenetic level, rescue from water symbolizes the exile of man to land. "One is also tempted," he wrote, "to explain the various deluge myths as a reversal, of a sort familiar to psychoanalysis, of the true state of affairs. The first and foremost danger encountered by organisms which were all originally water-inhabiting was not that of inundation but of dessication. The raising of Mount Ararat out of the waters of the flood would thus be not only a deliverance . . . but at the same time the original catastrophe which may have only later on been recast from the standpoint of land-dwellers."

THE KONA COAST, Big Island of Hawai'i, a bay some two miles across at the mouth and a mile or so deep, to which the dolphins make almost daily visits. They come, it appears, for respite from the predators of the open ocean, and/or simply to once more approach the land their ancestors left behind. Here in the bay, after a night of deep-sea feeding, the dolphins "sleep" in the clear, (almost) shark-free water, in extended periods of relative silence, that is, without the endless and necessary echolocating of their life in the open ocean.

Ecotourism. Having flown thousands of miles to commune with wild dolphins, she swims out alone into the deep blue wearing mask, snorkel, fins, yellow waterproof camera tied to her wrist. Periodically she stops to hoot like an owl, as loud as she can, hoots as echoes returning from the rocky north wall of the bay, her goal being to summon the dolphins. Though it is true that various Polynesian and Melanesian cultures have been able to call both wild sharks and turtles, she perhaps does not realize that the dolphins may well have been coming to this spot for thousands of years; that she'll make the dolphins appear in the sense that hooting before sunrise will make the sun come up; that with their sonar the dolphins can hear—see—her slow progress, her labored breathing, her intermittent kicking, legs fatigued so soon, blisters forming under the fins. That with echolocation the dolphins read her lungs. Her heart.

Somehow, perhaps a third of a mile offshore, she loses the mask and snorkel, had thought they would float, but then, as she starts to adjust the strap, lets go for a moment and they start to sink, turning slowly, slowly, dropping into the endless blue/blue-black. She dives after them, but doesn't take enough breath. Returns to the surface, sees that mask and snorkel are spiraling down and down. Too far to dive now. Suddenly she realizes she needs the mask and snorkel, must have them. Feels the enormous distance back to shore; feels fear.

By all rights, it should have been a dolphin that saved her. But no, it was a member of the killer species who came paddling in her direction, to whose petrochemically produced kayak she clung, breathing hard, panic very slowly subsiding.

I MPARADISED. Verb transitive—to put in or as in paradise, to make supremely happy. A cold day, for Hawai'i, below 70, water temp 73, 74. An old woman shivers, tests the water. "This isn't paradise," she says. No. But not for want of trying. From the Hawaiian Tel white pages: Paradise Finance/Paradise Implants/Paradise Laundromat/Paradise Termite and Pest Control/Paradise Towing/Paradise Used Furniture.

Whites in the tropics. The price of warm water. On the airplane to Hawai'i, a sea change: one departs as writer, Californian from Boston, son of a doctor and a poet, but deplanes at Honolulu as, poof!, a mainland *haole.*

Beachcomber, beachbum, hippie, expatriate, trader, missionary. Outcast of the islands. Sadhu with surfboard. Variations on the theme. "Going native," for instance. Sailor Jean Cabri in the Marquesas in the late eighteenth century, who, returned against his will to his own kind, was covered with tattoos, had practiced sorcery and traded the corpses of men killed in battle (though refraining from eating them himself), had almost forgotten how to speak French. (Cabri subsequently taught swimming to Russian marines, at the end of his life was performing in country fairs.)

Other variations. Melville, who stayed so short a time in the tropics but realized this was not his world. Nonetheless then marketing such exotic terrain to the folks back home. Twain, who loved Hawai'i but could never return, who promised a novel of Hawai'i but did not write it. Stevenson, who extended his life by heading for warm water. Nineteenth-century historian Henry Adams, who loathed the South Pacific. Gauguin; Malinowski; Conrad; Mead: whites making much capital by delivering the *mana* of the primitive.

These archetypes, these ghosts, these options/parallels/inevitables. These cards on the table. The sense of whites in the postcolonial tropics that their legitimacy is now waning. Has waned. That their very presence evokes, implies a history of sustained physical or administrative violence; requires explanation, defense. There is a movement now for sovereignty for the Hawaiian people—it is one hundred years since the illegal overthrow of the Hawaiian monarchy—and, despite the tourism and condos and golf courses, despite the collective denial, there is in Hawai'i a *soupçon* of Rhodesia before Zimbawe.

In the late sixties, one often heard the term *Polynesian paralysis*, a disease that still threatened whites in the American tropics, for which there was no inoculation. "The adult European," wrote R. A. Derrick of Fiji's high humidity and small variations in temperature, "tends to become enervated, and tired of his environment." And, lamented Baron Anatole Von Hugel, a nineteenth-century collector in Fiji: "I am much disheartened at the thought of so many months having passed and my having done so little—absolutely nothing—in them." Von Hugel's companion, he complains, is "so acclimatised" that he "cannot realise the value of time more than anyone does here, and tomorrow seems always better than today for anything which has to be done . . . to live and vegetate, as so many of the whites do here, is by no means so impossible a habit to fall into as one would have expected."

One cure was to transform the tropics into something more familiar. Imported food/traffic jams/air conditioning/pollution/a cash economy/housing so expensive that many locals now work two jobs to make ends meet. For example, at a surf break out past Sandy Beach, near the juice wagons, there's a Hawaiian who dreams of the water at night, but gets to it only on Sunday mornings. He and the wife both working. He does construction days and physical therapy graveyard shifts at a hospital, went to a Pentecostal school. "We were evil," he says of his education. In San Francisco, one remembers, there are now no bohemians in the Bohemian Club.

Whites in Hawai'i. Twice-told tales in a place where history is being revised, reread, reimagined. By 1819, some forty years after Cook's first landfall in Hawai'i, there had been much interaction between Hawaiians and the European sailors, and many of the *kapus*—religious restrictions—had been eased, ignored, or selectively enforced, if only in dealings with whites or on board their ships. More, influential Hawaiians may always have had latitude in interpreting the gods' requirements. When Kamehameha I died in 1819, his designated heir, Liholiho, had for years been under the guardianship of Ka'ahumanu, foremost of Kamehameha's many wives. Ka'ahumanu now declared her intention to share power with Liholiho. Beyond the issues of her personal freedom and political influence, perhaps acknowledging what Hawaiians now held to be true—that the epidemics since the arrival of whites argued that the ways of old no longer obtained—Ka'ahumanu announced she would no longer observe the *kapu* system. Needing an alliance with her to survive as king, Liholiho finally sat down to eat with female chiefs, thus repudiating the precept that the eating of food was for men—

and men only—a communion with the gods. Soon the temples were torn down, the images of the gods burned.

A year later, the first American Protestant missionaries caught sight of the volcanos of the Big Island, their timing extraordinary, something like Pizarro's in Peru, Cortez's in the land of Montezuma. Their arrival was in part inspired by the life and memoir of a young Hawaiian orphan, Opukaha'ia, who in 1809 sailed via Canton and the Cape of Good Hope to New York. Henry Obookiah, as he was now called, learned to speak and read English, and over time, not without relapses, he also learned to say—to think?—"I'm a poor heathen"; "I'm a poor unworthy sinner"; and "Time is precious." Though it was Obookiah's plan to return to Hawai'i, he died of typhus, "without fear / with a heavenly smile on his / countenance and glory in his soul."

In Hawai'i several years later, the American missionaries Obookiah inspired courted Ka'ahumanu, who one day came to the mission house directly from the ocean and sat on the settee, "as if from Eden, in the dress of innocence." Over the course of her gradual conversion, Ka'ahumanu traveled the islands telling the people about the new religion. (As Silverman writes, "a woman, nonsacred, in her traditional world she had not been allowed involvement in religious matters. Yet her political position . . . induced the missionaries to give her the central role in encouraging Christianity, a role they would never have allowed a woman in their own country.") Though not yet baptized—her marriage to the son of her late husband was one impediment— Ka'ahumanu came to believe that all commoners should learn to read, to keep the Sabbath, to worship the Christian God, and to obey His law. Nonetheless, Ka'ahumanu picked her own way: even as she enforced the new law against adultery, she took a young *haole* as her lover. She was single now, the missionaries' notion of sexual chastity simply not hers.

Before her death, Ka'ahumanu continued to speak of Christianity to the people, and also outlawed dancing of all kinds. In 1832, on her death bed, Ka'ahumanu "in a firm voice repeated two lines of a native hymn composed from the 51st Psalm: *Eia no au, e Iesu, E, / E nana oluoulu mai.* Here am I o Jesus, / O, Look this way in compassion."

Continuities, ties. The house in which Obookiah died is apparently still standing, his gravestone still there to be read. The places he lived in, visited, studied at, continue on without him: Yale; Andover, Massachusetts; Bradford Academy; Hollis, New Hampshire; Canaan, Connecticut; Amherst, Massachusetts. These are places I have been, have spent time in. I was born and raised in Boston, know the sweltering summers, the psychedelic humidity and heat and leafy greenness, the low, gray heartbreak of winter, the occasionally pellucid clarity of autumn, the mud of spring. I know snow/slush/sleet. I grew up under the thumb of Protestant New England, the blue laws of my childhood closing Boston down tight as a drum every interminable Sunday. And, though I have no blood or religious connection to the missionaries, New England seldom fails to leave its stamp on those in its precincts, can assimilate—can make New Englanders of—even Hawaiians. When I was a child you read Edith Wharton's *Ethan Frome,* that saga of doomed lovers with winter closing in. The message not passion but the price of passion. By the time I was in high school I frequently worked as a musician in Boston area Protestant churches. Waiting for the next hymn, shivering in the cold, looking down from the organ loft, I could see that Hope, Freedom, Sex, Escape were not at all the promise of those buildings, those sermons, those faces. Not in this life, in any case.

Not surprisingly, then, I had a disturbing sense of coming home when I first arrived in Hawai'i as the sixties became seventies, encountering not only the tropics and Polynesia but the architecture of my childhood in various nineteenth-century Hawaiian churches and homes. There was Red Sand beach and its ironwood trees, there was Haleakalā and Kaupō Gap, there were the *mahus* in women's clothing singing in falsetto at a baby *lūau* on Moloka'i—clearly here was another place, another people, another set of premises. With all this, however, there was the overlay of, the undertone of, a too-familiar reality and set of proprieties. Between them, the nineteenth-century New England missionaries and traders had powerfully influenced—had in time taken control of—the life of these islands. Six thousand miles from the home I'd long since left behind, I was forced to remember what it was in my childhood I had bridled against, incorporated, sought to purge from my heart.

The period in which I first visited the outer islands was the end of the plantation era, many of the country towns still sleepy backwaters, a period also marked by the arrival of a wave of young whites in search of Eden, migrants often uninterested in or actively determined to ignore the human history of the islands, content simply to reach a further California. If the hippie *haoles* could seem selfish or callous, narcissistic in their obsession with religious search or diet, on the other hand many of them lived close to the land or the water, simply and quietly, came to know the physical environment very well indeed. Had, in some cases, an extraordinary if occasionally self-destructive yearning to merge with it. At the least, their impulse to purity or pleasure or Nature forced one to define one's own mission in the islands, and, inevitably, to take stock of the white continuum that had begun with the traders and missionaries. I spent many mornings at the ocean, many afternoons in the Wailuku public library.

Years later, in Honolulu, I'd go down to the beach each day for an hour. Often, I'd see the same very tan young woman in a folding chair listening to a Sony Walkman, bouncing with the beat, smearing herself with another round of oil. Always she'd be wearing the barest of bikinis, her breasts pneumatic to a degree not in all likelihood envisioned by the Almighty. Thus exposed, she nonetheless radiated the desire to be left alone, and so I did my best. Occasionally she'd take out a joint and light up, and I'd smell the sweet smoke, watch her legs moving hard to the invisible drummer's tempos. One day, after weeks of seeing me there, perhaps appreciating that I'd done no more than nod hello, one day she offered a joint to share with me. Subsequently, we'd exchange a few words, and, finally, had a conversation. Her name was Rose, I learned, which I might have guessed from the tattoo on her left biceps. It turned out Rose was a "dancer," and before I could stop myself I asked, "What kind of dancer?" though I nearly bit my tongue trying to keep the words from coming out of my mouth. Too late: Rose seemed disappointed—I'd shown such admirable restraint thus far—but nonetheless continued the conversation. She'd been a coke freak, it turned out, down to ninety pounds (a girlfriend died from an overdose), she worked as a stripper only a few months at a time, could get a job anywhere she wanted, and . . . she was from Boston. From East Boston, actually. Italian-Irish; raised on the third floor of one of the old three-deckers near Logan Airport; she'd gone to the beach every summer in Winthrop, her father was a fireman who often knocked her around, particularly when she began to get interested in boys. Her father who had recently remarried a woman younger than Rose.

Now this may seem odd, but on that beach in Honolulu that day, Pacific stretching out before us, Rose, well-oiled, toking on her joint—it may seem odd, but of everything about Rose—from tattoo to bikini to Sony Walkman—what engaged me most was that she was from Boston. I felt a special connection, being able as I thought to read what had shaped her, what she'd emerged from, what she carried in her heart. Knowing the streets she'd walked, schools she'd attended, faces she'd seen, the voices still in her ear. What she'd confronted, ducked, escaped, would be nostalgic for. Talking to Rose, I could see the North End of my college days, of Rose's childhood. Very close, the North End was, to East Boston, the other end of the Sumner Tunnel. Just twenty, I was going out with a woman who lived in the North End, on snowy evenings would ride my motorcycle down the narrow streets, tar glistening, past the old tight graveyards overlooking Boston Harbor—Paul Revere's house was down here, the church the famous lantern had hung in (one if by land / two if by sea)—and past the Italian markets with rabbits dangling in the window. I'd spend the night, radiator clanking, clanking, but then be very, very careful not to hold her hand in public, not to put my arm around her as we made a slow progress through the neighborhood stopping for vegetables, bread, or pasta at each small shop, not to appear to be her lover lest her reputation be . . . shot.

Boston. Honolulu, on a beach with Rose, sun beating down, the healing waters close by, a lone frigate bird sailing high overhead. Willy-nilly, Rose and I took our place in the continuum of New Englanders who'd come to the islands, people who would in time become either more or less New Englanders—asserting their distance from or hunger to come closer to an environment and a people so very unlike what had been left behind.

S HE HEARD IT, she says, as a riddle. *A bell rings. A man dies. A bell rings.* You can ask questions to get at the riddle, as she had to. For example, is there more than one bell? Did the man die on land? It turns out the "riddle" would be very hard to solve without clues, even once you establish that the man died in the water, and that at least one of the bells was a ship's bell.

The story of the "riddle" is, finally, that there was a blind man, a very good swimmer, who swam in the ocean every day. Apparently the blind man's practice was to put an alarm clock in the sand set to ring after a half hour. He'd hear the bell ring and would come in, guided by the sound. One day, however, a ship was passing just before the half-hour mark, and the bell the blind man heard—sound travels well in the water, she explains—was the ship's, so the blind man began to follow the ship out to sea. This, she says, is a true story, that is, the person who told the "riddle" to her said it was a true story.

Blind man in the water, alarm clock on the beach. Improbable; unsatisfying. Nonetheless, the idea of a blind swimmer following a ship's bell out to sea . . . now *this* image lingers, provokes. One can see the blind man in the swell, stroke after stroke after stroke. One can hear the ship's bell. One can see the blind man, a very strong swimmer, ship pulling away, blind man ever more distant from shore. Ever more alone.

God, what a fate. Blind and alone at sea. Surely a nightmare, to be in water without knowing where the shore is, how far. Not to know what else is in there with you.

Thinking about it, one searches for firm ground. At the very least, all this is good reason to knock on wood at the thought of being blind, to thank one's lucky stars. Good reason too, one concludes, not to swim in the ocean on moonless nights. Yet is there not something more that disturbs in this story? The sense that, somehow, all of us are blind, all of us alone at sea?

NoT VERY FAR from some famous breaks, his game is surfboards, selling to tourists, buying from locals. Using power psychology techniques, gleaned from investing programs advertised on cable TV, to find the weak spot in each customer. The fantasies of the buyers—all those big waves to ride—and the often desperate need for cash of the sellers. Has-beens. Wannabes. Surf-movie wet dreams or memories of adolescence. One seller comes in late. "Life's like football," he tells the man, pushing a finger at his chest, "and you just really dropped the ball." Browbeating works, he's found. Get 'em backpedaling. Pathetic, he often thinks, every last one of 'em. He wears a bathing suit to work, but never, ever goes near the beach.

Dreamtime (versus what Aboriginal artist Trevor Nickolls has called *Machinetime*). Down at the seawall not long before sunrise, very low tide, sound of waves breaking on the reef, an enormous but lozenge-thin full moon being lowered toward the horizon, flush of daybreak coming both around and over Diamond Head, swath of white light on green ocean. Swath of white light. "And did this these feet . . ." If Christ in fact once walked on water, surely he could have done worse than to choose such a path. But if He did, He left something here still undone. In a building nearby, not more than thirty feet from the ocean, a tenant was recently stabbed to death. He'd apparently met someone at a bar, had invited him home, was killed. No sign of break-in, fight, or ransacking, police announced. A twenty-one-year-old Marine was charged with second-degree murder.

The indifferent sea, the implacable sea? Matthew Arnold's "estranging sea"; Yeats's sea with its "murderous innocence." The ocean, it is true, is full of death, but it has also been said that what distinguishes humans from fish is that we do not consume our own kind.

T HE PHOTOGRAPHER Wayne Levin underwater, seeking to deepen the mystery. Fins, goggles, and a camera strapped to his wrist, often down five to thirty feet, in the path of a collapsing wave, reef perilously close, or with a forty-five to fifty-foot humpback surfacing nearby, yet again at Makapu'u in the clouds and fog of aquatic turbulence or in the deep, still, blue-black of Kealakekua Bay.

Twenty years of this, and it has been, as they say, a learning experience. "As a large outside wave approaches," Levin explains, "you dive under and feel the pull of it passing over you, and then as the wave breaks the spray blown off the top of the wave comes down like an instant of heavy rain." Or, "The key to survival in rough water is that there is tranquility down below. Of course, this creates a problem, since inevitably you have to return to the surface." Photographing surfers, he says, is true reflex photography—"I just have to react and trust my reactions. Not only do the surfers move through my visible space in a matter of seconds, but that space itself is in constant flux, with a visibility of one hundred feet in one instant and three feet the next." And, "The waves are extremely steep at Half Point as they break over a shallow reef. I am about twenty feet toward the shore from a group of board surfers and body surfers. The coral reef is about four feet beneath me. A wave approaches and one of the boards shoots down the face, heading directly toward me. I take one exposure, then dive for safety, but the oncoming wave has sucked out much of the water; the depth is now only two or three feet. Clinging to the reef, I feel the wake from the skeg [fin] of the board as it passes inches from my head. Wheeling around, I hit the shutter as the board skims across the face of the wave." And, of a school of *aholehole* sighted outside at Hanauma Bay in somewhat calmer water, he says: "It was like a wall of fish. At times it would encircle me. I'd swim through it and it would open up like a tunnel."

Searching to photograph dolphins and humpbacks ("The whale stuff has been difficult," he reports, laconically), Levin's commitment has as usual been labor intensive, requiring him to swim great distances, to paddle his kayak for miles. "I was a little reluctant to use weight belts in a bottomless ocean," he reports, though of course he ends up doing so in an effort to get down deep quickly, to be able to photograph marine mammals at their level or even from below. "Dolphins move at human speed or even faster," he notes, "but whales move in what seems to be slow motion. Even when they breach it seems that they are taking forever, rising simply on pure power."

The photographer searching the horizon for sign of a whale's blow, for days at a time finding nothing at all, intervals between occurances of life surprising, almost confusing. Scanning the waves for some swirl that might suggest recent movement in the water, for bubbles that might indicate life below, for shadows just beneath surface, focusing and refocusing his eyes to discern what is no more substantial than a wisp of smoke, since "if something is visually persistent in the water it is usually human or dead." And, "If you're not looking within forty-five degrees of where a whale or dolphin comes up you won't see it unless you hear it. You really have to be looking at one to see it. The result is that you really start seeing—imagining—things."

Yet of course all Levin's water photographs are seeing as a form of imagining. "The large marine creatures," he says, "fill me with awe. In their presence I'm transposed into a mythological realm, and they are the spirits or gods of this world." Feeling this even as he swims on in search of them, paddles in search of them, waits for them in the broiling sun. Submerges in pursuit yet another time. This fusion of close observation of the physical world, a passionate specificity, and the heart moved to wonder.

Mastery, surrender. The photographer in the dangerous 'Alenuihaha Channel, getting overwhelmed by the current. "I paddled hard," Levin says. "It seemed the first half hour I wasn't making any progress toward land. There was a little bit of doubt. I wouldn't say I panicked, but I felt fear." Or, in the water with whales: "There is something frightening about proximity to something that big, also the knowledge that you are in the presence of a superior being." Or, on sharks (laconically, again): "I haven't seen any recently." And, finally: "Of course I realize how helpless I am out there. Each time I go out I'm placing my life in the hands of something infinitely more powerful than I am. It's only by the grace of the sea that I return."

The photographer, pondering, after so many years in the water. Standing on shore, sun hot on his shoulders, staring at the deep blue, reflected light blinding, disorienting. "The surface, this boundary between water and air, constantly undulating, reflecting on each side the world it faces while obscuring the other world. Giving the illusion that reality remains the same as far as the mind can see, that even the other side of that mirror is more of the familiar, if a somewhat distorted version. But can two worlds so unalike really have the same gods? The congregations of worshippers are certainly different! I often think of the obsession of science fiction with other dimensions, some utterly different universe that coexists in the same space as our own or is parallel to it, an invisible membrane dividing these two universes, a membrane that occasionally allows passage through. At the least, I often feel like Alice entering Wonderland. Down and down I go."

Portrait of the artist: late forties, five-foot-eight, 140 pounds, pure will at least where the ocean is concerned. (Only) one good eye, sleeps on a . . . waterbed. Wife and infant daughter, garden teeming with bananas, avocados, corn, radishes, peppers, pineapples, mosquitos. Dawn chorus of roosters just down the way, everything leafy and green, greener. A dazzlingly battered, nearly antique Toyota station wagon being loaded yet one more time with water gear. Find the door that opens . . . This being the artist at work on the Kona Coast of the island of Hawai'i, a rural area where the forces of nature are inescapably imminent, land still being born through volcanic eruptions, ocean always reshaping, reclaiming, that land. Beneath and in the wind shadow of the huge, long, high wall of Mauna Loa, under the vast vault of the sky, in this boundless ocean, the photographer is the Loch Ness monster of his own photos, sea creature just beyond our field of vision. Diving down yet one more time as broad shafts of light radiate up from below, hair streaming behind as he disappears into the murk, wake of air bubbles trailing from his fins, the contrails of his energy. (To keep near him in the water, this recommendation: play the infant dolphin, stay close to what would be his dorsal fin, ride on the pressure waves created by his movement in the water. No worry, it will take only the occasional flip of your fluke.) Back at the surface, a breath before another passage through the liquid mirror, the photographer becomes one of the chimeras he follows, is transformed into the kind of mirage he stalks. See—imagine—Levin in his kayak in search of a whale, trying to locate that huge needle in that huger haystack, paddling into the sunset and so beyond our capacity to make him out any longer, paddling relentlessly toward the horizon until he is no more than a filament in one's eye, as hard to apprehend or to contain as any force of nature, the artist now at least as elusive as what he has for so long, so intensely, pursued.

T HE LACRYMAL APPARATUS: ducts and glands producing and transporting that saline secretion between the eye and lid which ordinarily passes through the nasolachrymal duct into the nose. As for other questions . . .

- Is how much people cry a constant for all cultures?
- Is it crying if there are no tears?
- Why do women shed more tears than men? Or do they?
- How about American males? Is it true they cry more in middle age—the death of parents, one's own bones creaking?
- Tears of rage?
- Weep not, want not?
- What about old age? Do tears multiply with regrets? Diminish with dessication? Increase with incontinence?
- When people cry in mourning, are they speeding the deceased home to the sea?

PREPARATIONS for the descent. February in northern California. Heading out for my morning double cappuccino, I see the plum trees budding, pumping, aching to bloom. Obviously, one should be here for them every day. To live if not forever, then locally, the more so in corporate/cable TV/postmodern times. Era of the inauthentic, of soft-core, of metacommunication. Poses: video violence; video sex. Despite the opportunity to see more of the Pacific, I hear myself constructing arguments against travel: how many places can one really understand, after all? A man tells me he travels to avoid being parochial. Surely a matter best settled between himself and himself; in the privacy of his own home, perhaps.

Packing, nonetheless. Farewelling the known: this cottage, these small truths. Poet Philip Larkin, that sometimes vicious stick-in-the-mud, playing the provincial. Along with Kipling's "Mandalay" ("For the temple-bells are callin', an' it's there that I would be— / By the old Moulmein Pagoda, lookin' lazy at the sea"), I photocopy some Larkin to take down to the South Pacific: "At death, you break up: the bits that were you / Start speeding away from each other for ever / With no one to see.

It's only oblivion, true: / We had it before, but then it was going to end."

Recovering from minor surgery, just in time to let go of the small, unspeakable, counterproductive, bone-marrow realization that Someday It Will All Be Over. To celebrate, I don my whaletooth fishhook necklace, invoking Maui, the demigod who fished up various Pacific Islands (and who was en route to conquering Death by heading up Her vagina until She crossed Her legs, the end of the end of Death). Thus attired, I attempt to prevision Fiji: in Suva it's twenty hours earlier and tomorrow.

And leaving behind . . . Well, a week before I depart, when a friend with a BMW tells me owning it has not made him happy, I suggest he give it to me, but no, *not* having the BMW made him even less happy. And so I leave behind: the homeless. Batman. The Sharper Image Catalogue, our apparently endless hunger for more things, for the expensive, miniaturized, dys- or pseudo-functional. Also leaving behind: AIDS. (Though, I learn, there are already two cases in the Pacific Island nation of Kiribati, population seventy-thousand, an incidence which can be construed to mean that by, say, the year 2050 everyone there will have AIDS). Leaving behind AT&T's "Reach Out and Touch Someone." By phone, they mean to say.

The day before I depart, I meet an academic who has spent much time in the South Pacific, whose ambitions and woes— Ph.D. research, divorce—have been played out in the tiny communities of Polynesia and Melanesia. Thinking of how, despite the vast water distances between nations, expatriates willy-nilly come to know of and gossip about each other, she gives a bitter grin: "the Pacific puddle," she says.

So down, down, to the antipodes (an-TIP-o-des: situated on the opposite side of the globe; things diametrically opposite). According to fourteenth-century travel writer Sir John Mandeville, after passing through the Great Sea Ocean one reaches a land where people go naked all the time, believing that nothing natural is ugly ("for they say God made Adam and Eve naked"); where there is no marriage (because God said to Adam and Eve, "Increase and multiply"); where everything is common property; where—*uh-oh*—they eat human flesh "more gladly than any other." Also, in the antipodes, islands where the people do not speak but "hiss to one another like adders"; where there are "ugly fellows whose upper lip is so big that when they sleep in the sun they cover all their faces with it." Islands also of dwarfs, of people who have no tongues, of hermaphrodites who, when they use their male member, *beget* children, and, when they use the female, *bear* children. There is in addition, Mandeville explains, an island "where the people live just on the smell of a kind of apple; and if they lost that smell, they would die forthwith."

Thus informed, I depart. Singer Paul Simon: "These are the days of miracles and wonders, this is a long-distance call." Our enormous plane heading south and west through the night, falling down across the equator. On a screen before us: miles-achieved/miles-to-destination/time-to-destination/map graphic constantly replotting our position. Forget the banal miracle of flight, think relative scale: somewhere below the weight of three hundred and fifty of us and all our gear, just this one plane among many daily planes, there is the island nation of Western Samoa (150 thousand souls?). And Tonga (100 thousand souls?). ("The horror! The horror!" Kurtz cries in Conrad's *Heart of Darkness*. Referring to the sight of tourists, no doubt.)

Fiji: Viti Levu, overlooking Suva harbor. Downslope, the art deco Burns Philp building, container ships behind the enormous municipal market, cable ship at anchor, the harbor, the reefs. Across the bay, large jagged green mountains topped with rain clouds; the volcanic plug called Joske's Thumb; plume of smoke from the cement plant in Lami; the island of Beqa (pron. "Mbenga") in the distance. In Mandeville's antipodes, there is an island where the ocean which surrounds it "seems so high above the land that it looks . . . as if it hung in the air on the point of falling and covering the earth; and that is a marvellous thing, as the prophet says, *Mirabiles elaciones maris,* that is, 'Wonderful are the risings of the sea.' " Here in Suva, however, though there are sometimes hurricanes at this time of year, it is only rainy season in a rainy place, 125 inches per year, usually a windless straight drop, first mist and then a sudden downpour, and then . . . nothing at all. Not surprisingly, enormous umbrellas with a rainbow of colors are common in Suva.

The antipodes, if not yet as far south as the Antipodes Islands (below New Zealand, uninhabited by humans, home of herds of fur seals). Here in Fiji, no obvious inversions: no one's walking upside down, no fish flying. But where, so to speak, are people coming from? Fijians are Melanesian; to an American, Fijians are blacks, but here, what does that mean? Swedish sociologist Gunnar Myrdal, some fifty years ago, saw clearly the enormous distance between America's rhetoric of justice and equal opportunity and the ongoing treatment of its largest minority. And Alexis de Tocqueville, more than a century before Myrdal, wrote that the abolition of slavery would "increase the repugnance of the white population for the blacks . . . The danger of a conflict between the white and the black inhabitants perpetually haunts the imagination of the Americans, like a painful dream." I remember visiting New York City one winter, suddenly realizing I'd misread the terms of the place. A group of black teenagers approaching at early dusk in the bottom of Penn Station, somehow not another soul around. *Scaree* for me; just a tease for them. Or a day in rural Virginia, in the truly tropical heat and humidity, cicadas racheting, shooting hoops with nine young black men. "Give the white boy the ball, give the white boy the ball," one of them kept shouting after I made my first score. But in Fiji? Upstairs at Luckie Eddie's, a nightclub on Victoria Parade, the dancers under the strobes are singing along with Michael Jackson—"If you want to be my baby it doesn't matter if you're black or white." The crowd predominantly Fijian, a few whites ("Europeans," the euphemism), some "part-Europeans" (i.e., part-Fijians), a few Indians, a few Chinese. There seems to be no hostility in the air: truly antipodean, if so. (Where people are coming from. Though here I become a European, the Australians and New Zealanders—most of the whites—are of course also foreign to me, despite the functional illusion of common language. For a few days, I read lips to help parse what they say. But beyond intelligibility, there is the question of the known. The All-Blacks, for instance. Totemic to them, an imponderable to me.)

Scheme of things racial aside, Suva is a city—of seventy to two hundred thousand, depending on how much of the outlying areas one includes. In Suva there are taxis (I soon sit in front, to the driver's left, but keep forgetting to look to the right when stepping off the curb); street lights (though the city is underlit, by American standards); stoplights (not many). Banks, several large office buildings, a massive government building, perhaps ten nightclubs, some thirty or forty restaurants. Narrow side streets full of duty-free shops. Computers. Air conditioners. A few elevators. One escalator. Australian entrepreneurs seeking the obligatory Fijian partners for their ventures. Price Waterhouse, its pamphlet "Doing Business in Fiji." If all this seems normal enough, the toys in the American Embassy suggest that it is an alien normality. Weapons detector, buzzer releasing locked door, enormous stereo speakers, these are, at the least, awesomely expensive here. Guards, for instance—i.e., humans—cheaper, more consonant with the Fijian economy.

A city—what else might it be?—Suva gives one the feeling that the familiar is at best an analogue, this even as one hears Sinead O'Connor's brilliantly neuresthenic rendition of Prince's "Nothing Compares 2 U" on the radio. "Economic dualism"; "urbanization without industrialization." "Proletarianization," people migrating in from the outer islands; ongoing "monetization" of an economy that had few cash exchanges. "Development of a secular materialist society." But not quite yet. (Development also euphemism, for neo-colonialization: the price of copra keeps falling relative to the price of fuel, for instance.) Suva thus a kind of Potemkin village, an as-if, a quasi-city. There is no background roar in Suva; at night and on Sundays, it is deserted. Fijians gone, packed in those smoking Leyland buses that look like something out of a children's book, dispersing out to a way of life that no more than interfaces with Suva: out to subsistence agriculture, the margin of the cash economy, to communal, clan living in the village. Or: in Suva, one looks again at the dense vegetation and realizes it is not shrubbery but someone's small "plantation," that nearly everywhere in Suva food—taro, cassava, breadfruit, mango, papaya—is grown for personal consumption. Or, in a nearby church a choir of Fijians is singing Handel's *Messiah* a cappella. But down the road, well within the city limits, surrounded by suburban homes, is a Fijian village, land commonly held, no fences separating house from house, and on that land an utterly nonwestern set of assumptions about rank, family, the role of money. As John O'Carroll puts it, in Suva "communalism and private property exist side-by-side," requiring from "Europeans" an at least partial state of psychological accomodation or . . . denial. The kind of ongoing anomaly that could create unease, encourage heavy drinking, for instance, induce a kind of chronic polyphrenia. *Gone Troppo.*

Suva in February: intense heat, humidity; mosquitoes (and the hint of dengue fever); dogs barking nonstop through the night; post-coup Orwellian political dialogue; a constitution that utterly mocks civil liberties. Government-controlled TV being introduced: one channel. Paul Simon's "Graceland" on the radio: "There is a girl in New York City / Who calls herself the human trampoline / And sometimes when I'm falling, / flying / Or tumbling in turmoil I say / Oh, so this is what she means."

If this city is somehow not a city, I think, what of this water? That reef I survey, for instance, wreck always out there on its side, high and dry. Suva harbor is a lagoon. In May 1884, a ship called the *Syria,* fifty-eight days and thousands of successful miles out of Calcutta, approached Viti Levu bringing laborers from India—coolies, was the term—to work the sugar cane. (Embarking on what they referred to as the Great Water, unable to observe caste restrictions, Indians lost their very place in the social order.) In sight of shore, the *Syria* struck the reef. According to Doctor William MacGregor, who led the rescue effort, few of the Indians knew how to swim. "People falling, fainting, drowning all around one; the cries for instant help, uttered in an unknown tongue, but emphasized by looks of agony and the horror of impending death." Ten men were left on a sandbank by overloaded rescue boats as night fell, were never found again. Sixty-five people died.

Suva and water: Nubukalou stream, which runs through the center of town past Morris Hedstrom, the major department store, is polluted. Some people tell me the entire bay within the reef is polluted. They may be right: I contract an ear infection swimming in Lami. It is true, there are no real beaches for miles in either direction, but still the absence of any visible shore or water culture in Suva is striking, disturbing. Only rarely a fisherman in sight, almost never a swimmer. Even if the bottom is dead coral or shallow mangrove terrain . . . nobody in the water, nobody? There is of course the Royal Suva Yacht Club a mile down the road in Walu Bay, but no one seems to swim from the dock there either, and the boats, dazzlingly expensive in Fijian terms—so much gear, so much painting and scraping to maintain, races to compete in—only seem like a further "European" alienation from the water they float on. Scuba diving is also popular among expatriates in Suva, but there is a long launch ride out to the reefs, and again, so much gear and technology and cost. I know that in Fiji there are places where villagers have for centuries chanted to call sharks and turtles. I know these people live by the water, fish as part of daily life. Even at Nukulau island, out in the harbor, one spots sea snakes among the mangroves in the 85-degree shoal water, sees Fijians fishing ("Cargo: We Deliver the Goods," reads one man's T-shirt). But in Suva, in Suva there is little sign of this. No sign, in fact, except for the impromptu fish market on the side of Nubukalou stream near the municipal market. There, Fridays and Saturdays, the big market days, women in from the villages sit selling smoke-cured octopus, clusters of land and sea crabs, strings of small fish. Fishermen, Yamaha skiffs tied to the seawall, offer enormous lobster, parrotfish, prawns. And turtles: sometimes speared, usually netted. This ancient order of reptiles. A very large one on its back, the lower shell, the plastron, already cut away, turtle being slowly, deliberately, butchered out while still alive, great heart still beating, pumping as the turtle urinates, urinates again, shell now a bowl for its own blood. Turtle meat is greatly valued here—was it once for chiefs only?—and worth a great deal to the fishermen. There is no refrigeration; this may be how villagers best make use of the meat. Turtles themselves are often omnivores—grass, seaweed, mollusks, jellyfish. But still, in the incredible heat and humidity, alien to this place as I am, under the spell of an antibiotic for my ear infection from the polluted water, I turn away from this perfunctory but merciless slaughter. And turn back again to watch. And turn away again.

Later in the afternoon, trade winds blowing from the south and east, I go to the home of a man who's lived for years in the South Pacific. Modest, hard-working, wry, an outdoorsman, a man who knows he has a terminal disease. Who is in some way already dead, given his precise knowledge of his fate, talking to me from the Other Side. The good news is that there is no point wasting money on the search for treatment. His half-Fijian son, a palm tree freak, into the names of the many varieties of palms and orchids and shells the way American nine-year-olds are into baseball statistics, plays in the next room. Around us as we talk are beautiful shells, rare shells: his wife is a diver and collector.

Sunset, a sudden rain squall and cooling. "It'll be clear tomorrow morning," the man tells me. He knows this environment. It is not fair; it is merely the random nature of travel and the traveler's moody eye; the essential point of a place is often missed, obscured, ignored by the visitor; I will soon be out on remote islands with Fijian villagers, witnessing their matter-of-fact expertise in harvesting marine life from living reefs, reefs teeming with life. But in Suva this day, in this city that is not quite a city, talking with this man whose decline and approaching death—*evaporation,* almost—leaves me thinking both of my good fortune and our common condition. . . . Oh, on this particular day in the antipodes, by water that is not at all the water that heals, things are if not upside down then really not quite what they should be.

STEAMER LANE, a break at Santa Cruz, California. Summer surfing, air temp 75, but everyone in full wet suit—the water some twenty degrees colder. Lots of long boards, giving the feeling of a fifties dance party, an Edsel convention.

Pelicans cruising by the surfers. Sea otters, the occasional seal. The possibility of great white sharks attracted by the sea lion colony just up the coast. (Recent attack just south of Ano Nuevo: surfer survived.) No wind, and even more glassy because of the kelp beds. The wave today thick, broad, strong yet forgiving, everyone heading right because a left would take you into the cliff.

The calm water, the recurring powerful wave rising up out of the flat ocean over and over again. An enormous long line of hundreds of seabirds just above the surface winging to and descending on a spot near the kelp beds. Barn swallows endlessly in and out of their nests under the eaves of the lighthouse. And the waves within waves, the endless undulations of aquatic animals.

Sound waves, light waves. "The singular force of time," John Cheever wrote, "through which one seems to swim." Or, as Joseph Brodsky argues, "Water equals time," is "fully synonymous with time," even as we are "partly synonymous with water": thoughts, emotions, handwriting, blood, all have a water pattern. Reflecting on Venice, Brodsky wrote: "Should the world be designated a genre, its main stylistic device would no doubt be water."

L̲ATE MAY, south swell up on O'ahu, in from the Antarctic, pumping, pumping, pumping, a miracle of nature, on the order of the Grand Canyon, even the breaks way offshore happening now, everyone with a piece of flotation larger than a chopstick out there on the waves. Lifeguards working overtime. Seen through binoculars, distance foreshortened, the falling surfers evoke the super slow-mo charge scene in *The Wild Bunch*, replay tumbles on TV football, the fight sequence blows in Scorcese's *Raging Bull*. A surfer starts to get tubed, for instance— to get covered by the curl of the breaking wave—but, poof, the tube closes down on him. Gone: God's fly swatter.

IN EARLY 1991, novelist Jerzy Kosinski was found dead in his bathtub, not drowned but asphyxiated by a plastic bag he'd tied around his head. Kosinski, who several decades before had fled Communist Poland, was the winner of a National Book Award. (A few years earlier it had been alleged that Kosinski's fiction was produced only with massive editorial help. Some of his defenders argued the charges were a Communist plot.)

Not long before his suicide, Kosinski produced a brief essay to accompany "Pools," an exhibition of paintings by well-known artists. In this essay, he writes that he'd had a fear of drowning from childhood in Poland, when "I was pushed under the ice as a prank by village kids." Despite this fear, Kosinski says he was always still able to swim, even "enjoyed" it, but felt nonetheless "terrified of water closing over me." (In Kosinski's first novel, *The Painted Bird*, the young protagonist is thrown into a cesspool, a horror Kosinski told people was inflicted on him during World War II.)

At forty-nine, vacationing in Thailand, Kosinski saw a Buddhist monk floating upright in a swimming pool, "totally motionless . . . totally and peacefully afloat." As Kosinski recounts the episode, the monk—while floating—explained that the trick is "being oneself . . . To drown is to do something to water." The monk "then let the imperceptibly gentle current of the water and wind carry him away from the pool's edge, toward the pool's very center, away from me."

Inspired, Kosinski then began to study yoga techniques to increase both lung capacity and the amount of oxygen in the blood, which, he felt, would result in added buoyancy. Eventually, Kosinski was apparently able to rest motionless in the water in various yoga poses, a skill producing "varied reactions of pure envy which I chose to perceive as tributes to my psychosomatic achievement."

What about all this? I see no reason to doubt Kosinski's special ability to float, though some parts of his story do make one wonder, or, induce disbelief. For instance, not only was the monk's repartee almost too suitably Zen-like, but the man must have indeed been buoyant to float away on so "imperceptible" a current and breeze. Nonetheless, I believe Kosinski may have in fact learned an unusual skill.

But at the level of water, so to speak, what kind of story is this, really? How does such floating compare, for instance, to the control and strength of water ballet? To the skills of competitive divers, competitive swimmers, water-polo players, pearl fishermen, body surfers? As for the "envy" of others when they see him floating in a lotus position (Kosinski often has the protagonists in his fiction trumping their adversaries) . . . If fear of water is the point, if Kosinski really wanted to be "drownless," what in fact had he learned about submission to what Conrad calls the "deep, deep element"? Put another way, that monk notwithstanding, what god of what sea would believe Kosinski was speaking of essential things?

Water destinations, destinies. Stowing, restowing gear on shipboard, a sense of almost instantaneous mildewing in the light rain and . . . once again land falls away. What promise this place held so short a time ago! The utter abruptness of leaving the known, under sail once more, a new life before us. Behind us, land receding as we lose the capacity to discern essential shape; the recent past distorted, already no more than illusion. Distance: memory's correlative. But of course more islands dead ahead. Yet another beach to cross for the first time. As the whole damn species had to do. Onward, then: the endless and ongoing present tense of life on the water.

The tropics: The Koro Sea, north up Somo Somo Strait past Viani Bay on a gently rolling south swell, ocean a long carpet of blue. Islands with coconut palms along the ridges, like Mohican haircuts, vegetation pushing right down to the high-water mark and even beyond, coconuts floating in toward shore already sprouting, ready to take root. At anchor, swell wrapping around the point into this small bay, boat pivoting, rocking, dropping, bucking, pitching, pulling. Goading, wracking. Island rising and falling through the companionway: we should be gimballed, like the stove. Willy-nilly one becomes a compass needle, floating, turning, searching.

The afterglow of sunset, a land breeze, deep, more than sweet. Vegetable fertility, stench of decomposing so rich that one wants to lie down and join in. (Too much work to lower the dinghy, too cool to swim to shore.) Later, owls hooting, moon waxing, boat still chafing, a hunger for stars, for the Southern Cross. We sleep, boat restless, restless, perhaps its karma (first owner killed by cane cutters hired by his wife and her boyfriend.)

Dawn, first light. Failing to make headway against the southeast trades, instead crossing Tasman Strait, north on a broad reach with following sea. Entering Budd Reef, a deep lagoon some twelve by five miles, its convoy of islands, camels' humps intermittently disappearing into the rain, or in different formations according to our angle and distance and the mist, the eye tricked, confounded. Thombia merging with Yanutha which merges with Yavu which may or may not appear to be part of what chart and compass tell us should be Raranitingga. . . . Mirages we seek to make out, to precise, to achieve; microworlds we will in time leave astern as sails fill, green turning gray, these forms dissolving in the haze.

GLASSY CONDITIONS, paddling out a hundred yards toward Tongg's, admiring/appreciating/savoring the glass, then after a few minutes sitting up to survey the break, to adjust my wet suit vest, take a breath. And there, beside me: life! A gecko, right on the surface, head up like a surfer's, four feet as outriggers. Immediately, questions: how did it get there? Did a branch fall into the water? And, how long can a gecko survive out on the waves?

Flattening the board by moving forward slightly, I swing the nose toward the gecko and then lift, raising the gecko onto a kind of terra firma. Is it relieved? No sign, but we both stay motionless, gently rising and falling together on the swell, until a wave sweeps the gecko back into the water. I maneuver it onto the board another time, lose it again. Repeat the sequence several times. Begin to ponder my choices. Try to bring the gecko back to shore to spare it from becoming a meal for fish or bird, to save it from becoming immobilized as the sun wanes (my theory being that geckos are coldblooded)? And what kind of gecko is it anyway? Is it a young gecko, whose mother repeatedly said, "Don't go near the water"? Wouldn't I want someone to save me in such conditions? And yet, here I am, *very* close to the break, and it will be hard to keep the gecko on my board. Hold it in one hand, perhaps, as I paddle in?

I weigh the choices, remember the many times I've freed moths, bees, even birds trapped inside my house. "An American Gandhi," I've often teased myself, going to the kitchen yet another time to get a cup and newspaper to trap a wasp in order to release it, to stop it from beating itself to death against the bathroom window. Teasing myself perhaps because I believe the act to be out of character. An American Gandhi! This though I know the great man had his limits, his faults, a crew of young girls to massage him in his old age. Gandhi. I look again at the glassy waves, the extraordinary clarity of their shape, consider— brood about—how little I like paddling. Not to mention back in and out again. Finally, finally, making my decision. Either way playing, if not God, then Poseidon.

T WO WATER PAINTINGS. From my childhood, as if always there in my parents' home, a given, a print of Hokusai's famous *Kanagawa-oki naimura* (Under the Wave off Kanagawa), done in the early nineteenth century, the artist then in his seventies, calling himself "Old Man Mad with Painting." Known as the Great Wave, this famous print has the three cargo boats of wretched oarsmen huddled over, holding on for dear life, cowering before the enormous towering wave with its tentacles of foam, a snow-covered Mount Fuji echoing the wave's colors far in the distance. Most of the water in the picture is in the sky, above the boats, about to engulf them, and we are right there to see it, very close.

Because I knew this painting from childhood, however, it was first of all simply an icon of the familiar. Whatever was depicted meant less than its sheer presence; it was part of what was domestic, routine, orderly, safe. Only years later, after the death of a second parent, bringing the print home with me, did I see it with new eyes, really took in the wave, the sailors' terror.

A second water painting. Just after college, in 1965, I became the close friend of a fellow whose field was Classics, for whom the legends of ancient Greece were relevant, true, awe inspiring.

His Dionysius—a free spirit, challenging order, not to be contained by mere politicians, the Dionysius of Euripides's *Bacchae*—became mine. The sixties just breaking when my friend and I met, this was a Dionysius made for the times, more than capable of rising to the coming madness, drugs/war/sexual license.

It was not until 1972 that I reached the Cyclades, spending time in and on the wine-dark sea, had occasion again and again to think of the kylix of the vase painter and potter Exekias (sixth century B.C.). On his well-known cup, a now-dull red represents both sea and sky, which have no boundary one from the other, and the bearded Dionysius—in black—apparently completely at ease, sails his tiny cetacean-ship, surrounded by seven dolphins, a vine heavy with grape clusters rising above and over the mast and single sail. The painting of course evokes the story of how Dionysius was seized by pirates but then revealed himself, the crew diving into the sea and turned into dolphins.

I've had a postcard with this kylix on it since the mid-sixties, keep it unframed but on display on a bookcase shelf in my study. Often, it evokes those years, the madness and passion of something close to a civil war in the United States, and the dissolution of boundaries allowed—forced—by mass drug use. Dionysius at work. Often, too, the card brings the Cycladic Greece of 1972 back to me, the goatherd's whistles, the donkey's groans, the Pleiades, green terraces and bare hillsides. And also evokes a time, after weeks and weeks of swimming for miles in the Aegean each day, when I almost drowned. Now, seeing Dionysius sailing along, dolphins jumping, I also think of the god's lack of fear, his utter ease in—on—that dull-red and undifferentiated sea and sky.

D (ROWNING IN) the sea of love. Soon after they met, one night they walked arm in arm on the long pier out on the bay, stopping every few minutes to embrace and kiss (at a suitable distance from the shark fishermen huddled in the cold by their coils of line and chain), sweep of water below and behind amplifying, extending, their falling in love.

Almost seven years later, she said, "We have to talk."

"Let's wait until next weekend," he replied, and on Sunday it was to the pier and the bay that they went. A bright morning, fog burning off by eleven, lots of families out with their children, Latinos, African-Americans, Chinese, Vietnamese, Anglos of various ethnicities and persuasions, Serbian to post-punk, the multicultural/multiracial northern California of the very late twentieth century.

When, as they walked, she asked him the question she'd waited to insist on getting an answer to, the question he'd long been avoiding, when she at long last demanded to know, he could not believe he was actually saying the words. The truth if not elicited then made feasible by the expanse of water, the space above it, the light. As if only such open water allowed him to give so much pain.

SEA HORSES. Dog fish. Goat fish. Mermen. In *The Compleat Angler*, Walton quotes Du Bartas: "God quicken'd in the sea, and in the rivers, / So many fishes of so many features, / That in the waters we may see all creatures, / Even all that on earth are to be found, / As if the world were in deep waters drown'd. / For seas (as well as skies) have sun, moon, stars."

In the *Kumulipo*, a Hawaiian creation chant, the sea life being born is paired with emerging life on shore: *ēkaha*, seaweed, with *ēkahakaha*, bird's-nest fern; *kō'ele*, seaweed, with *kō'ele'ele*, the long-jointed sugarcane. And, subsequently, *umaumalei*, eel and *'ūlei*, shrub; *weke* (mackerel) and *wauke*, a plant.

These parallels, correspondences. A conceit, perhaps, only an intellectual construct? Enter the reef waters of a tropic island. Ten yards off the beach, just below the surface, look down. Teeming . . . *forests, thickets* of staghorn, plate, brain, and mushroom coral; seafans; coral hard and soft. Green *Acorpora*, squirrelfish browsing. Rise toward the liquid mirror; emerge, look: hundreds of palms lining the beach, hundreds of palms also reflected, doubled, on the surface of the lagoon.

The ocean is closed.
　　　　—Sign at a Miami Beach hotel,
　　　　noted by Lewis Lapham.

W ENDELL RIDING HIGH on his ten-foot board that day
off Diamond Head, the two of us gently rising and falling on
the swell, lull in no hurry to end, Wendell speaking of the
headline in the morning paper: a sewage plant down the coast
had once again been dumping vast amounts of raw waste into
the ocean. Sewage, nuclear wastes, drift nets, the plan to build
new breakwaters and groins at Waikiki and to pour tons of sand
to "save" the beach. To kill the reefs, destroy the surf. "You
know," Wendell observes as we sit there, waiting for—being
there for—the next set, "you know, there is just no end to man's
greed."

Man's greed: "God gave Noah the rainbow sign, no more
water but the fire next time." Well, maybe not. Maybe water
once again. In the late 1960s, scientists came up with something

called polywater, which possessed a very low freezing temperature and a very high boiling point. There was apparently some initial fear that polywater, in contact with natural water, might take it over until the earth became completely unable to support life. This seems just the kind of thing that Vonnegut had in mind in *Cat's Cradle*'s famous ice-nine, a different kind of ice, which could "teach" ordinary water to stack and lock in a new way, to reform, to structure itself to melt at, say, 130 degrees Fahrenheit. Such a water as this, of course, would mean the end of all life on Earth.

CAPTIVE DOLPHINS. Bottlenose dolphins, *Tursiops traun-catus montagu,* with pink lower jaws, throats. "Hi, sweetheart," the director says to one of them as he passes the tank. The dolphins look incredibly vital, seem truly affectionate with him. (In the adjoining tank, the trainers, both women, are praising the dolphins for successfully completing a task, shouting with hyperbolic enthusiasm, like cheerleaders, or with the too-theatrical gusto of the parent of a young child: "Good girl, good girl.") In this facility, there is no "intrusive" study, and the director would prefer "elective captivity," allowing the dolphins to come and go at will over a low barrier, a system that has worked well elsewhere, if only he could get the funding and permits. In these times of tight budgets, however, the tanks are right beside the ocean but also absolutely removed. Of course the dolphins hear the surf, smell the salt air, see the stars and moon, but are actually closest to the bar right next door. Surely the dolphins have no choice but to listen to the rock music each night, perhaps even to the two drunk guys picking up two women by telling them dirty jokes as they wave to the waitress for yet another round.

Captive cetaceans. Karen Pryor, pioneer trainer of dolphins, points out that whenever "we humans have moved into a new habitat, we have tamed and made use of animals . . . whose skills in that environment exceed our own." (Pigs, camels, yaks, water buffalo, falcons, elephants, cormorants. And sheep, for example, which we have bred into a new kind of sheep.) Domestication, Pryor argues, is always a trade-off. "An animal gives up its freedom and wild companions and contributes produce or work of some sort; in return, it is fed and kept safe from predators, thus escaping the two biggest problems of life in the wild, going hungry and getting eaten. Many species have proved quite willing to make this bargain." *Quite willing:* Pryor's argument fails to make explicit that most captive dolphins have been taken in the wild, often violently (and that many of these dolphins then die of shock or survive only a short time); and the adaptation to captivity by such dolphins, however successful, is not initially freely chosen (think of the several conversions of Patty Hearst, for instance). Even love under such conditions, human to dolphin, is a form of coercion, response from dolphin to human tainted by the boundaries imposed. Still, with the development of programs to breed dolphins in captivity, Pryor's argument may carry more force.

Kenneth Norris approaches the issue somewhat differently, saying that Flipper, the TV star, and other captive cetaceans changed the public consciousness about dolphins, thus saving the species from extermination (by humans, needless to say). In this view, captive dolphins are at worst a sacrifice for the group, a small price to pay given, say, the annual slaughter of hundreds of thousands of dolphins by the tuna fisheries. This is a compelling argument from someone who has labored mightily for years to create legislation to save cetaceans. And yet . . . Norris is also a scientist who very much believes in the need for "data," for "controlled experiments." The word *control,* however, may be loaded in a way Norris does not intend, speaking to an impatience about information that does not lend itself to certain kinds of human hungers. The scientific method expresses a yearning for clarity, for "proof," for knowledge that is "replicable," that leads to . . . action. Are humans capable, however, of a calculus of apprehending living creatures? Does the possibility that we lack such a calculus suggest limits on how we "study" such creatures? Should we see even the language used as normative, rethink words if not premises?

At this particular dolphin research center, some fifteen years ago, two dolphins were "freed," that is, "kidnapped" and taken to the ocean and "released." (See Gavan Daws's extraordinary paper "Men, Dolphins, and Biography" on the human and cetacean protagonists.) Domesticated as they were, and without other dolphins to help them, they may have died quite soon, though this is not certain. What is certain is that for the director of the center it was an incredible loss. These were animals he knew well, cared for deeply. Animals on the observation of which his professional career had been built. As he puts it, years after the event, "They stole my dolphins." One can hear, still, the anger and the grief: "They stole my dolphins."

My car, my child, my life, my country, my God, my book, my heart, my family, my destiny. My friend, my body, my garden, my soul. My tree. My dog, my cat, my rabbit, my hamster, my cow; my lamb. My pig; my elephant. When referring to cetaceans, the possessive seems a not quite incomprehensible leap of language, but still, usage that will take some getting used to.

THE PAINTER. Raised in the home of quite secular middle class Jews, comfortably assimilated, in a southern California beach town in the fifties (his father a Bolshevik who fought in the Russian revolution before emigrating). Down to Argentina as an exchange student during high school—so many former Nazis there!—and on after college to Poland, a fellowship to study the origins of Polish abstract art (Warsaw in the early twentieth century somewhere on the road between Moscow's "Suprematists" and the European cultural center of Berlin). Then pursuing his own art as modernist and incipient postmodernist. Cardboard furniture, tables and benches, he fabricated for his house—oh transience! oh detritus! Also constructions, glass boxes containing images and objects to isolate and enclose meaning. Spare, this work, an approach to purity, getting at essence, if also not exactly teeming with life. At risk of being a bit clinical. For one painting, he built a wall in his studio and gridded off a canvas something like five by nine feet, the result being 21,012 squares which he painted by hand—gray—using a translucent medium with graphite as the pigment. Romantic minimalism, it could have been termed, a longing for an image anyone from any culture would be able to come to without impediment, the creation of an all-encompassing field, absolutely continuous, but each aspect articulated, so that the sum of all its moments could be the sum of . . . all possible moments, or . . . the world, you might say. The painter only years later beginning both to teach himself Hebrew and to study Torah, in the process, as if by an obvious corollary, approaching the essential vastness he aspired to in art by a quite specific source, by taking the measure of the Polish Yiddishkeit he'd arrived too late to see, painting elegies to the memories and ghosts of the Jews who'd lived in Poland for one thousand years, his oils shifting toward both warm and cool from the mix of deep and resonant reds and blues and dark browns, evoking the spirit of rolling fields, autumn haystacks, acrid coal smoke, Chopin and swans, winter's slush, "and the people themselves . . . a nation gone, vanished, not even buried."

What seems so remarkable about the painter, beyond the depth and range of his talents, is that unlike so many converts to no matter what faith, he has not needed to repudiate the life before conversion. Rather, it is as if the painter in him was waiting for him to find . . . God. (Jews, however, avoid saying the actual name of the ineffable out loud. Instead, one employs various indirections: *eheye asher eheye*, I-am-that-I-am [or, I-am-the-one-that-has-always-been-who-is-and-who-always-will-be]; *ha-shem* (the name); or, *maienei mayim haim*, the wellspring of living waters.

The painter at forty-five: At home on the Sabbath, old Testament beard, black yarmulke, having read the day's portion of Torah and some commentary in the Talmud, now talking about . . . *surfing*, about how as a child on the beach north of San Diego he started with an air mattress and, by age eleven, had a balsa board, single fin, redwood strip down the middle, purchased up the coast in Huntington Beach from Velzy/

Jacobs—was Jacobs a Jew? the painter now wonders. By the time the painter finished high school the new foam boards were coming in, technology emanating from aerospace people at Convair. Before departing, the painter built an eighteen-foot outrigger, the great Phil Edwards—the first man to surf Pipe-line!—a familiar figure around town and the painter's mentor for the boat. The painter smiling to remember the grace with which Phil Edwards could shape—construct—a surfboard.

Sitting in his living room, thinking of those days, the painter, full beard now very gray, suddenly jumps on to the coffee table, lands on his knees, yarmulke holding steady, and begins to paddle. Then, spotting the wave, he grasps the rails of the coffee table and, quick as a cat, springs to his feet, landing in a crouch without any discernible impact, goofy foot (right foot) forward, arms out for balance, now taking the drop, laughing, hooting. ("Straight-off Adolph," they'd call each other—incapable of making turns.) And then, moving forward on the coffee table, the painter extends his sandaled feet over the edge, hanging ten, accepts the applause, and, stepping back, hunches over in a Quasimoto (sic: surfspeak). More applause. Finally stalling the coffee table, pushing the nose up in the air by standing on the edge of the near end, and dismounting.

"Torah is water," they say (and people come to drink). They also say that the Talmud is like the sea. And, they say, "Come swim with us in the sea of the Talmud."

J UST OFF THE ISLAND of Kandavu, Fiji, south coast fringed with barrier reefs which eventually swing north to merge into the great Astrolabe reef. Southeast trades often driving heavy seas. Water blue until it turns electric green and then turquoise near the reef, white of breaking waves just beyond. Land here volcanic, densely vegetated; black-green, yellow-green. And signs of human life on this tiny island: mosquito nets, kerosene lanterns, cisterns, cook house, outhouse. Palusami being prepared for the earth oven: fern, taro leaves, banana leaves, onions, cassava, taro, grated coconut, corned beef. The dull metal thump of yangona being pounded for grog. This extended family, three generations and various nieces, nephews, cousins. The occasional shopping trip, over to the adjacent larger island by walking on the reef, heading for Low Chee's tiny store for fuel or tobacco. Or fishing from the skiff just inside the outer reef: large clams, octopus, the occasional shark passing, the younger men of the clan free diving with hand spears, deep, hour after hour.

Hsu Li, age eight and a half. In a crayoned picture before this trip, he'd envisioned Fiji: blue sky, blue "oshin," orange "quiksand," green "bush." "This is what I think fiji looks like," he wrote, lower case *f*, the *j* backwards, "but biger [sic]." Hsu Li on the beach digging for crabs, drinking from a coconut, staring as a foot-long sea cucumber ejects long sticky threads—and then intestines—from its anus to drive off or appease this predator. Hsu Li in the shallows, humming, stalking, startling yet another school of small fish, hundreds of them leaping up, cascading through the surface as they flee. Hsu Li looking up: terns diving, rising to juggle their catch in midair, frigate birds wheeling above, about to pursue. Hsu Li looking back at the island, palms like Fourth of July sparklers along the ridge. Hsu Li just offshore, snorkeling over the reef, still humming, chugging along, for the first time reaching the far side, dropoff so steep, bottom suddenly so very far below. Hsu Li now treading water with real force, chest well above the surface, jerking the snorkel out of his mouth, looking toward shore to see just how far it is. "I think," Hsu Li says to the grownup beside him, the very word grownup already consoling, facilitating understatement, "I think it's a little deep for me here."

> . . . in ancient times, you could sleep in the sea.
> —Paul Eluard

UBI SUNT? Older surfer in the south swell, driving left. An unmistakable stance, to anyone who has seen photos of the great surfers of the sixties, pictures of this man and others when they were eighteen/twenty/twenty-five. The good news is that this fellow is still in shape, still out there. And the other news? Oh, that he is no longer the young man he once was, whatever wisdom he's achieved along the way. *Où sont les vagues d'antan* . . . In the morning paper, four weekend water deaths are reported, one of them a man on the Big Island who "disappeared in the ocean."

Funeral of a surfer in Honolulu, canoes heading out off Sans Souci Beach to strew his ashes on the waves. Story of one of the last Micronesian master navigators, who not long ago apparently took his small sailing craft out for a last voyage and failed to return. All this evoking Queenqueg, who one gray morning told Ishmael "that while in Nantucket he had chanced to see certain little canoes of dark wood, like the rich warwood of his native isle; and upon enquiry he had learned that all whalemen who died in Nantucket were laid in those same dark canoes, and that the fancy of being so laid had much pleased him; for it was not unlike the custom of his own race, who, after embalming a dead warrior, stretched him out in his canoe, and so left him to be floated away to the starry archipelagoes; for not only do they believe that the stars are isles, but that far beyond all visible horizons, their own mild, uncontinented seas interflow with the blue heavens, and so form the white breakers of the milky way. He added, that he shuddered at the thought of being buried in his hammock, according to the usual sea custom, tossed like something vile to the death-devouring sharks. No: he desired a canoe like those of Nantucket, all the more congenial to him, being a whaleman, that like a whale-boat these coffin-canoes were without a keel; though that involved but uncertain steering, and much leeway adown the dim ages."

Once washed, Ivan Illich writes, the dead in traditional Indo-Germanic cultures journeyed until they waded or were ferried across a body of water which took away the memories of all who crossed. These memories were then carried to a well of remembrance named for Mnemosyne, mother of the Muses. Drinking from her waters, living mortals, coming back from a dream or vision, could recount what they had learned. "Philo says that by taking the place of a shadow the poet recollects the deeds which a dead man has forgotten. In this way the world of the living is constantly nourished by the flow from Mnemosyne's lap through which dream water ferries to the living those deeds that the shadows no long need." (Solitary drinker in the bar drowning his sorrows: drowning in memories.) (Souse: to plunge into water or other liquid, to steep, to pickle. Slang: to intoxicate.)

In early 1991, a seventy-two-year-old retired electrical engineer died while surfing off Spanish Beach in northern California. "That's what he did," his widow said. "He surfed. He'd just go out there and wait for the waves. If he had a profession, I guess that was it."

What a way to go, no? Right on the face of the waters. ("In the beginning God created the heavens and the earth. The earth was without form and void, and darkness was upon the face of the deep; and the Spirit of God was moving over the face of the waters.") When *I* die, please, scatter my ashes on the face of the waters. *Warm* waters, too, as I head off. Let me cycle and recycle in the tropics forever and ever, lest the residue of my flesh and bone cry out—ashes that were my teeth now chattering, ashes that were my lips now turning blue—lest the residue that was me haunt the living by crying out from the briny deep for . . . something like a wet suit against the dreadful chill, against the dreaded chill factor. No. Make it easy on all of us: let the waters be warm.

And don't mourn for me. I'll be in touch . . . when it rains. When it pours!

EDDIE AIKAU, the great Hawaiian surfer and waterman, died at sea in 1978. He'd been part of the crew aboard *Hokule'a*, a replica of the traditional Hawaiian sailing canoes. When the boat capsized in gale winds in the treacherous Moloka'i Channel, emergency rescue beacon lost and the craft perhaps drifting out of air and shipping lanes, Aikau took his surfboard and paddled for help toward Lāna'i, some twelve miles off. Twelve miles in a storm at sea? It might as well have been twelve thousand. Perhaps Aikau was mistaken: there is an axiom among sailors that you stay with the boat; in the end, his shipmates were all rescued. Yet Aikau was a man of enormous courage, and, believing he could save the lives of his crewmates, he went. As usual—an aggressive surfer even among the big-wave dare-devils—not holding back from nightmarish risk.

Now there's an annual tournament in Aikau's name at Wai-mea Bay. The competition proceeds, however, only if and when the waves are twenty feet or more, the great waves Aikau was a master at surfing. Often this means the tournament waits for weeks to begin, or does not begin at all, an untelegenic if not anachronistic insistence on standards and accommodation to Nature that must try the sponsor's patience.

Driving around the island of O'ahu, one sometimes sees a bumper sticker on cars and pickups driven by locals, a kind of ambiguous mantra combining reminder and enjoinder for those pausing at the brink, about to take the drop, on the waves or in life: *Eddie would go.*

$\mathbb{R}$EADING WATER. In his recent and remarkably mean-spirited account of traveling in the Pacific, *The Happy Isles of Oceania*, Paul Theroux is disabled with misery in the form of self-pity. Ah, lost love. The wife that got away, though in more than five hundred pages Theroux cannot bring himself to tell the reader just what went wrong. (In *My Secret History*, however, an earlier novel, Theroux's protagonist is a cuckolded travel writer who then betrays his wife.) Which still leaves Theroux bitter and alone, speaking no indigenous Pacific tongue as he wanders in the clan- and family-oriented islands needing desperately to be acknowledged, valued. Loved. "They had no interest whatsoever in me," he writes of some Tongans in Vava'u. "They were incurious, indifferent, probably mocking." This drives Theroux crazy, has him imagining how under other circumstances "they would have groveled and paid fond attention to my butt."

Writing of the Trobriand Islanders, Theroux can't stand his place in Pacific history, has himself saying to some boys, "Don't call me *dim-dim*. I come from America." Poor Theroux-in-Oceania, one more *palangi* tourist with money to blow, arriving by plane and rent-a-car and making long-distance calls in a region of subsistence farmers. Little cash here, but also very little *anomie.* Theroux thus some kind of breathing parable of atomistic capitalism, the solitary self with credit card. Theroux camping on private property whenever it suits him—"The idea of trespassing excited me"—and then disappearing to still another island nation, dazzlingly rich by islanders' standards but denying he's rich when they ask: an occupational hazard of wealth, to feel poor. To poor-mouth. Theroux special among tourists—if at all—for having a skin too thin to withstand Polynesian teasing.

Theroux, yuppie boatman in his folding kayak, toting Walkman and wine. What a devolution in the two hundred years since Captain Cook! Theroux, however, like the Cook of the last voyage, enraged by insolent natives, albeit politically correct on French nuclear testing and Japanese resorts. Taking moral credit for opinions of no great personal cost to him, opinions that too easily deflect appraisal to Theroux's own behavior. In fact, Theroux seems happiest when there are no natives to have to deal with, or when, as in Hawai'i, they have been disenfranchised and suppressed, leaving the paddling tourist free to savor environment-as-paradise.

The Happy Isles of Oceania is thus Theroux's revenge on Pacific Islanders, consonant with how he's (re)lived his life in previous books, making a virtue of truculence, caricaturizing, diminishing, many of those he encounters. Truly stealing their magic, not, as Theroux would have it, because he's a writer and that's what writers do, but because he's cast himself as the George Steinbrenner or Spiro Agnew of travel writers. On drinking kava, a ceremony with such ancient resonances: "I sat and clapped a little." And of Tongans: "They were usually late, unapologetic, envious, abrupt, lazy, mocking, quarrelsome, and peculiarly sadistic to their children." Not satisfied with forever giving himself the best lines in the arguments he records—

writing as wish fulfillment—Theroux keeps checking to see if the natives actually eat dog; is obsessed with their size and weight—hearing the chafing of thighs, he says; and, his essential psychological dynamic, looking for get-back. "I liked hearing stories of Polynesian seasickness." And, "I had assumed that, being Polynesians, they would be puking their guts out." For Theroux, people whose ancestors reached their island homes by sailing vessel should now, generations later, be comfortable on the open ocean. Theroux gloats, of course, because they're sick and he's not. (In *My Secret History*, Theroux's travel writer shoots his wife's lover with a urine-filled squirt gun.)

Should Pacific Islanders read Theroux's sloppily repetitive narrative, should they see him laboring to implicate the reader in his slanders, they may not deplore what happened to Theroux when he reached O'ahu. "On my first swim in Hawaii . . .," Theroux writes, "I was yanked by the undertow [sic], carried past the surf zone, and swept into a strong current almost a mile [sic] from my towel. I swam hard upstream [sic] for an hour [sic] and finally struggled ashore on sharp rocks, where I was lacerated and shaken . . . people said this happened to newcomers all the time."

Well, not to all newcomers, actually. Were Theroux telling this story about others, he'd argue that such a fate is for those who've made insufficient effort to understand the Pacific.

W ATER DAYS, early September, after a summer of small surf.

· No waves and high wind, or sudden waves too far to reach or too steep to ride without damage to board, self. Everything conspiring against surfing, as if the ocean (herself) had re- solved to be difficult, contrary. Fickle. Finally one can only head in, knowing, of course, that conditions will immediately improve, another instance of the surfer's odd intimacy with the waves, the perennial lover's quarrel.

· Truly, totally, flat; sky flat as well. No wind, leaving one not calm but . . . becalmed. A sudden moment of terrible doubt—talk about tropical depression!—making one won- der if the water ever did really offer power, solace, joy. (Consoled by language, by the idea of the *re*form, as surfers call it, accent on the first syllable. When the wave, apparently almost spent, gathers its powers and rises to break again in its progress to shore. The *re*form. I've always liked the sound of this use of the word—endless, the innovative music of living English—but am now also cheered by the idea of something summoning up new force within sight, reach, of certain termination.)

· Tut, they call him, a king in the water, standing by the map of the world on his office wall. "Storms down here by New Zealand," he says, "started several days ago. Swell should be up to the south shore any time." He tells me this with such easy certainty that I head home, rush out to the sea wall just before sunset, and sure enough, it's beginning to pump, the break known as Old Man's starting to go off. White water everywhere. A special promise in the air; you can almost hear surfers all over the island readying their gear. Except that, an hour later, night falling, the swell seems to have subsided. When, at 5:30 the next morning, I check it out again, Tut's swell is, sadly, still on its way.

· Incredibly hot and humid, nothing up from New Zealand, but a hurricane is six hundred miles south of O'ahu. Tut predicts a large south swell, as does everyone else.

· Dawn patrol, very hot, very humid, hazy, glassy. Not a breath of air. Surf popping, pounding, all along the south shore, white on green. Surf's up and with it a concomitant public health crisis: so many, many people will be calling in sick today.

· The eye of the hurricane itself just missing O'ahu. High winds, enormous surf, the waves vast but disorganized, confused, white water as far as the eye can see. Few if any surfers out in this fray, it seems. Except the Kaua'i man whose boat went down, finally found about eight to ten miles offshore clinging to a six-foot ice chest. As the headline in the local paper put it, a true rider on the storm.

CALL ME QUEEQUEG. One is not always at one's best. There have been times on land, particularly after too many days in our smog-filled postmodern urban centers, when the human capacity for affection and ingenuity has seemed to fail to hold its own with the human capacity for . . . well, you know. This may be a form of species fatigue, a special hazard of *Homo sapiens* in maturity, the kind of thing that sends Gulliver, back at last in the land of the Yahoos, out to his stable for hours yearning for the horselike Houyhnhnms, those creatures of true reason. In fact, when first restored to humankind, picked up by a ship, Gulliver is so revulsed that he plans to go overboard and swim for his life. Even years later Gulliver writes, "My Reconcilement to the Yahoo-kind in general might not be so difficult, if they would be content with those Vices and Follies only which Nature hath entitled them to. I am not in the least provoked at the sight of a Lawyer, a Pick-pocket, a Colonel, a Fool, a Lord, a Gamster, a Politician, a Whore-munger, a Physician, an Evidence, a Suborner, an Attorney, a Traytor, or the like . . . But, when I behold a Lump of Deformity, and Diseases both in Body and Mind, smitten with Pride . . ."

In such a state of dismay, one may seek to return to what

Melville called "the watery part of world." One thinks of Verne's brilliant and cultivated Captain Nemo, free in his submarine from the power of the despots who destroyed his country and family, free to avenge their loss, to be a benefactor of radical causes. Until, that is, the maelstrom consumes him and his crew. It being true for all of us that there have been times in or on the ocean when all one feels is threat, the ocean not singing but snarling. Its message? That there is no point in trying to escape, nothing to be gained in trying to be safe, in being too conscious. In being conscious at all. There is, for instance, no wit in the water. No respect for, say, the language of James Joyce. This is the ocean as Nature speaking, death the bottom line. (This is also the flip side of the ocean's siren song, the one that inveigled back into the brine reptiles and mammals which had already safely made it onto shore. Various reptiles, nearly 200 million years ago, and several waves of mammals beginning some 60 million years ago.)

Imperfect creatures, creatures of aspiration, inadequately or too well evolved—though surely some kind of success story—nonetheless we are completely at home in neither environment ("When men come to like a sea-life," Samuel Johnson said, "they are not fit to live on land.") Leaving us, often, in turmoil, and yearning. As Melville's Ishmael says at the opening of *Moby Dick*, "Whenever I find myself growing grim about the mouth; whenever it is a damp, drizzly November in my soul; whenever I find myself involuntarily pausing before coffin warehouses, and bringing up the rear of every funeral I meet; and especially whenever my hypos get such an upper hand of me, that it requires a strong moral principle to prevent myself from deliberately stepping into the street, and methodically knocking people's hats off—then I account it high time to get to sea as soon as I can." Where, we remember, Ishmael was not entirely in his element.

ONGG'S YET AGAIN, sunset, trades dropping off, an occasional random splash evoking the recent series of shark attacks, incoming sets ever more difficult to discern. Nearby, Carey from Kaimukī continues his thirty-year obsession, today, minimalist and miniaturist, reading and riding the nuances of a small wave all the way to shore as if to establish that this vortex too is worthy of consideration. Watching Carey as I have so many times, I conclude yet again that no one here surfs so intently, or with more grace. Just before this particular ride, both of us backlit by the afterglow, Carey was asking my opinion of the writing of Mishima.

Ginelle, nearby, in her late teens, as always wearing cut-off Levi's and a halter top, is about to head in. "Getting dark," she observes, paddling past on her short board. Not much given to talk, Ginelle, but a warm spirit with a bright smile. Ginelle and I have surfed at the same time of day here for several years: we share this place—exchanging appraisals of the waves, responding to a rainbow or sight of a dolphin—though seldom with more than a few words. Seeing Carey carefully sculpting a rill, I look over at Ginelle, and, improbably, hear myself hum a line from Dylan's "Girl from the North Country," "where the winds hit heavy, on the borderline." For a moment I remember early Dylan, so young, so slight, walking down that street in lower Manhattan; the sixties; the mainland. All the lives I've led that were not on these waves. Squinting, trying to make out the approaching set, blueblack sky ever less blue, it comes to me that here there is so much that need not be said. But then, words once more making themselves known, having their say, I grin at this thought: Ginelle, in the waning twilight, form ever less clear, Ginelle becoming . . . generic.

FROM A DISTANCE, the island looks like a Hershey's kiss: crater of an extinct volcano, a mile across. An opening a few hundred yards wide, bordered by reefs, on the northeast corner, salt lake within, its steep lava sides lined with mangroves. Above, incredibly dense vegetation.

What water gods bring me here? How trace the path? Begin with Exodus and the Red Sea? Sing of the River Jordan, the rivers of Babylon? Invoke grandparents crossing the Atlantic in steerage? On this trip alone, I'd flown five thousand miles. Sailed for days. Rowed this dinghy into the wind and swell to the point of exhaustion. Talk about sea level! Bailing, bailing. And could these damned oars—dowels! so little face did they have in the water—be functional, or merely some misguided tribute to Captain Bligh? Finally hauling the dinghy along the shore to make better headway. Losing a toenail.

Inside the crater the water is murky, warm. Amazingly still, after surfing the dinghy through the waves at the mouth of the gap. Coral along the crater wall, diving with mask and snorkel to take a look, and there, down below, a large shell, brown and white. *Homo sapiens*, hunter: the shell's fate and mine intersect. I think about leaving it, though I have the ordinary desire to acquire signs and significations of where I've been. Or is it that I am compelled by this particular object, its very gestalt stimulating an appropriate response? Whichever, I can't claim to be entirely against possessions, am an eager accumulator of black T-shirts, for instance, preferably with surf motif. I do, however, live simply by some people's standards, know too well how soon the pleasure of objects can pall. (How much I've divested myself of over the years, even my father's gold-headed walking stick. I inherited the impulse in my maternal genes, my mother notorious for getting rid of things once we four children were off to college, though it's also true that after she died we were surprised by just how much she'd held on to. Her term papers from high school?)

As for actually trying to get the shell, it's on a coral shelf about twenty-five feet down. Twice I dive and miss it, my pursuit less than ardent because odds are that it is living. To take will be to kill, and I have seen enough unnecessary dying in my time. That is, I may be the beneficiary of the death of the cattle or chickens or fish whose flesh I eat, but I respect vegetarians, have often truly resolved to become one . . . soon. Or so I recall as I head down a third time after the shell—a cowrie, I now see—dropping and retrieving it, then kicking my way back up toward the ceiling of the surface with some urgency. It would hardly do to suffocate for love of—through reflex need of; because of an almost casual hunger for?—a shell, would it?

Whatever was alive about the cowrie died and decomposed the next week as I sailed the Koro Sea. The smell—stench, truly—was extraordinary. There is a kind of lizard that birds will not eat because its particular coloration serves to warn that its flesh has a bitter taste. Generation after generation, birds stay away. In the case of cowries it seemed I was being taught a similar lesson, though of course I was hardly the first human to go after them. As a species, we are perhaps stubborn nonlearners. By way of penance, in any case, I resolved to do some research about what I'd acquired. Killed to possess.

Though the shell seemed large when I'd first beheld it twenty five feet below, it was only a bit more than three inches long, two and a half inches wide, and two inches high. It had the defining aperture, the long slot lined with ridges or teeth, and mottled spots of various sizes and shades of brown on white. A Tiger cowrie, though, as Hsu Li points out, it would more appropriately be called a Leopard cowrie.

Cowries, it turns out, are mollusks, invertebrates—animals without backbones—from the Latin *mollis,* soft, and most are algal grazers and most have shells (but not the octopus, for instance). Cowries are gastropods, one of the major classes of mollusks, along with snails, abalones, limpets, and conchs, among others. They have a visceral lump, containing most of the body organs; a lower head and foot which can be extended from the shell; and a mantle, a fleshy lobe containing the respiratory organs and also secreting the shell, pigments for which are taken from the mollusk's food (though there can be variations, the color patterns are genetically inherited). In cowries the sexes are separate, males injecting sperm into a sac in the female, which then lays fifty to one hundred eggs.

Humans have been eating mollusks since time immemorial, since antiquity cultivating and making purple dye from mollusks or using them as lime for fertilizer, and, particularly in the Pacific, fabricating tools, weapons, and fishing lures from them. Cowries have functioned as money in China, New Guinea, West Africa, and India (the word cowrie comes from the Hindi *kauri*). According to Safer and Gill, cowries "have circulated as currency in more places in the world than any coin." (It is of course hard to counterfeit a cowrie, though like any currency they are

subject to inflation.) Cowries were worn only by married woman ,
of the Turkana people in East Africa; signified wealth for the
Kuba of Zaire; and warriors in the Admiralty Islands were
entitled to wear an egg cowrie on the head of the penis. For the
Yoruba, cowries symbolize the white gods, whose powers are
life-giving, cool, and balanced, enhancing social stability. In
many cultures cowries have been worn as protective amulet
against the evil eye. In Fiji, virgins wear the white cowrie.

Cowries: the Diluculum cowrie, Great White-spotted cowrie,
the Clandestine cowrie, the Ocellate cowrie of Ceylon. For
collectors: Fulton's and Broderip's cowries from South Africa,
Barclay's cowrie from the Indian Ocean, the Surinam cowrie
from Brazil. The incredibly rare Leucodon and Prince cowries.
And then the quite common Tiger cowrie, the living creature I
dived to retrieve.

Hamilton-Patterson argues that "the more that people
become urbanized, the more they want about them talismans of
nature . . . marks of pilgrimage, like religious relics . . . Many
of these talismans come from the sea. They are tokens of lineage
and are to *Homo* what a family crest is to an aristocrat." For
Hamilton-Patterson, "this importing from one universe to another, from water to air, is invariably fatal. Nothing looks as
dead as a seashell in suburbia." *Souvenirs,* he argues, inevitably
become *memento mori.* This has the ring of truth, but, perhaps, at
the cost of overstatement. There is of course the sheer beauty
of some shells, dead or alive. And their symbolic power, cowrie
as vagina, for instance. Further, Hamilton-Patterson may under-
value the degree to which even a dead cowrie can evoke our
connection to its former world. To our lost world. Or simply
to any world beyond our reach.

Beyond this, it is perhaps not simply the cowrie's beauty but
our transformation of it that is essential to us. Speaking of Tiger

cowries, R. Tucker Abbot writes that "During the early 1900's, they were shipped from Zanzibar by the ton and sold at eastern American beach resorts, usually with the Lord's Prayer etched in the top." Which surely makes a certain sense to me. In a tiny village on a small island in the Koro Sea near that crater shaped like a Hershey's kiss, at nightfall in a tin-roofed house in which everyone was closely related, even the transvestite son-become-daughter safe in the bosom of the clan, not long before the kava was prepared, kerosene lamps at last being lit . . . In this village and in that house, my generous host sang a beautiful version of Bob Marley's reggae "No Woman, No Cry," everyone in for the chorus. And later that night, sky dense with stars as big as snowballs, many, many kava bowls later my host gave me a Tiger cowrie. On which he had, yes, painstakingly inscribed the Lord's Prayer.

T HE WIND SPEAKS the message of the sun to the sea," writes Drew Campion, "and the sea transmits it on through waves. The wave is the messenger, water the medium."

On the east side of the Big Island of Hawai'i, rain endless, 400 inches a year, soft, quiet, calming. Falling, dropping. Just north of Hilo at Honoli'i park in the afternoon humidity, mosquitoes swarming, the surfers jump into the cold water of Honoli'i Stream—a river, really—and are carried out right to the break. Conservation of energy.

Surfers as centaurs, as matadors. Teenage girl springing to her feet up off the board: Minoan dancer vaulting the horns of a bull. The ideal of the great waterman, the master surfer who has no commercial ties, surfs for the thing itself, who does not search for the waves but is, rather, found by them. Syncopation of the surfer, against the beat of the wave. Surfing is carving, they say; surfing is shredding. Surfers and time, slowing the wave down, speeding it up. The recurring mystery of moving toward the approaching wave instead of fleeing from it. Then taking the drop, trying not to wipe out. Impact zone. Boneyard.

At Mākaha on O'ahu, several older surfers on long boards sweep back and forth, elegantly, deliberately, like dinosaur herons or cranes from the Pleistocene, kids on short boards playing like porpoises, doing 360's as they hit the backwash from the shorebreak off the steep beach, and then, unbelievably, not stopping but surfing the backwash out against the flow, weaving through the incoming human traffic. Such artistry eliciting more and more and more from the waves until, in from so unutterably far away, the waves finally *expire*. As they would have anyway, this exuberant grace a gain without sacrifice of anyone or anything, a rare—impossible?—interaction of humans and the environment. Beyond the laws of physics: nothing lost.

These children at play, singing the song of the sea. What Whitman called the "inbound urge" of the waves. Pulse of the planet. This light, this air. As Keats wrote, "The moving waters at their priestlike task of pure ablution."

One's life passes before one's eyes. That is, just how much of your life would you give to be in such a medium in such a way?

ABOUT THE AUTHOR

Recipient of Guggenheim and National Endowment fellowships for his fiction, Thomas Farber has been Visiting Distinguished Writer at the University of Hawai'i, a Fulbright Scholar for Pacific Island Studies, and Visiting Fellow at the East-West Center.